CHICAGO PUBLIC LIBRARY
WRIGHTWOOD - ASHBURN BRANCH
8530 S. KEDZIE 60652

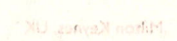

Avoiding The Path To: Teenage Suicide

Alain Simon Tuggle

Bloomington, IN  Milton Keynes, UK
authorHOUSE

AuthorHouse™
1663 Liberty Drive, Suite 200
Bloomington, IN 47403
www.authorhouse.com
Phone: 1-800-839-8640

AuthorHouse™ UK Ltd.
500 Avebury Boulevard
Central Milton Keynes, MK9 2BE
www.authorhouse.co.uk
Phone: 08001974150

© 2006 Alain Simon Tuggle. All rights reserved.

No part of this book may be reproduced, stored in a retrieval system, or transmitted by any means without the written permission of the author.

First published by AuthorHouse 6/20/2006

ISBN: 1-4259-3366-1 (sc)

Printed in the United States of America
Bloomington, Indiana

This book is printed on acid-free paper.

Contact Alain Simon Tuggle at   www.malibumud.com

Introduction

I believe that teenage suicide is 100% avoidable and preventable. I also know for a fact, that for some teenagers, suicide is the only answer they feel they have to obtain peace. I wrote this book to save the lives of children, and to keep families from exploding due to the loss of a son or a daughter because of suicide.

All the pictures, drawings, and poems that I put in this book were made after my suicide attempts. Like this book, none of what you see in front of you would have ever happened, if my suicide attempts were successful. I pray that this book gets in the hands of those that need it most.

Index

Page 1:   Teen Advice

Page 45:   Advice to Parents

Page 85:   My life Story

Page 133: In Closing

I dedicate this book to my father John Tuggle, Jamie, Mike, Dino and Jethro.

I thank you for keeping me alive!!!

To Friends and Family
Again the sun wakes me from my dreams.
The harder life gets, the harder life seems.
Yesterdays pain is just tomorrows sad memories.
So I wait for time and life to roll on beside me ,to guide me
    and show me my way.Through the sad tomorrows and the
    pain of   yesterday.
So I wait for the light to show me a sign.

Please god give me peace in my mind.

I now strive for a happy, and peaceful tomorrow

As I walk away from pain and hurt from my past.
I still long for the love that will last.
For now I smile as I feel the warmth of the sun.
There is strength in the light of a new day.
It's the love of my family and friends that make me feel this
    way.
Those people who stand by my side.
The people that are along for the long ride.
To these people, my family and friends, I say thank you and
    I love you.

                    Alain Tuggle   Feb 4 1991

Teen Advice

This book is geared toward showing troubled teenagers a way to look past the pains of today and see a better, pain-free tomorrow. There is a tomorrow out there for all teenagers, but you have to get past being a troubled teenager to get to this brighter tomorrow. I know that being a troubled teenager is not the easiest thing to overcome, but it can be overcome and that's what this book is about.

Yes, some of the things I say here are just plain common sense, but there are times in your life that you'll become blind to common sense. When you can't see life clearly through your anger, hate, frustration or depression, then you become desperate and common sense is thrown right out the window. As a former teenager, who is now 38 years old, I had problems that seemed so endless I tried to take my own life. I do know and remember how teenagers feel first-hand, when it comes to wanting to commit suicide. I know there are times that suicide is the only thing that makes sense in order to take away the pain. I also know how you can overcome this feeling of wanting to commit suicide. Teenagers, I say to you that you need to read this book with an open mind, as do your parents. What I mean by open mind is to not think for a minute that you know everything about everything, and therefore feel that you have nothing more you need to learn in order to survive in this world. The fact is, as a teenager, your life experience is limited because of your age or how many years you've actually been on this planet; so. please let yourself take in some blunt and in-your-face information. This information is meant to let you know that you are not alone and there is help to get you through the difficult times. I hope that you can find the help you need in this book and through the suggestions within it.

I'm crying out to you now; so, if there's no one else out there crying out to you, then let me be the one. I want you to be able to save yourself exactly like I did when I was a teenager with problems that seemed to have no end and no escape. There was no escape and, seemingly, no end to my problems. After years and years of problems, I dug down deep and I found inner strength with the help of my friends in order to make it through the toughest years of my life. You don't know me at the moment, but by the time you're done reading this book, you will.

In this book, I laid out my heart and soul for you. I did this in order to, hopefully, give a different perspective than just some off-the-shelf psychobabble from someone who has never felt what it's like to want to commit suicide every day of their childhood. I know this feeling all to well and I'm sorry to say that, statistically, there are thousands of teenagers who feel this same way. If you are a teenager reading this, I want you to know that I'm begging you to stay alive. Stay alive for your own sake. Having problems and getting through them is all a part of life, but, for some reason including hormone changes, it feels harder to go through when we are teenagers. Whatever your problem, "SUICIDE" is the wrong answer. As someone once said;

"SUICIDE IS A PERMANENT SOLUTION TO A TEMPORARY PROBLEM."

You need to reach down within yourself and stay alive, hang tough, stay strong and persevere. When you have the right tools and the right guidance to use those tools, life can be a lot easier to get through. This book is all about showing you a way to find your inner strength. A "POWER" so strong that you can overcome anything -- any obstacle, any hurdle, or any mountain that comes your way in life. You can overcome these problems at any age from 14 to 18; you just need the tools to help you and these tools come in the form of knowledge. The teenage years will be some of the most incredible years of your life. They should not to be wasted on "SUICIDE" for any reason, not for a bad report card, a break up with a girl or boyfriend, because you're not popular in school or you have a zit on your face. Suicide has no purpose or reason, not even for hate of one or both parents.

You may feel that there has to be a better life. You may look at your friends and wish you had what they have, a more loving mother or father, a nicer brother or sister. Whatever it is you wish for, you won't get it through suicide. You need to find a way to make tomorrow better than today, if the problems of today are bringing you down. Just know that there is no tomorrow with suicide as an answer for today.

Suicide ends all your dreams.

One of the main purposes for this book, is to motivate you to follow your dreams, whatever they may be. Follow your dreams to become anything you want in life. As you go through life and learn how to use all the tools that are before you, the future can be endless.

There is no future in SUICIDE!!!

BELIEVE IN YOURSELF!"

You need to "believe in yourself." It sounds simple to do, and I know, first hand, that it isn't as easy to do as it sounds. You may already know it isn't easy to believe in yourself.

It took me years to believe in myself and the things in life that I do with my art, work, relationships with my friends, family and women. Looking back on when I was in my teens, I realize that I didn't believe in myself or the things that I did, if I didn't have my friend's approval. I think I felt this way because I was always criticized by my mother, never able to feel that I met her approval. All I came to want was the approval of my friends, which took the place of my mother's approval.

There were times that I didn't believe enough in myself to go out on a limb and take a chance on something that could teach me or show me a different way of life. I share this so that you don't make the same mistake I made as you journey through the early years of your life.

If you feel something in you that drives you to do something like wanting to make new friends, try a new sport, or travel the world, then you need to go out on a limb and go for it. There are times in your life that you get the chance to do things, but for some unfathomable reason you might pass up that chance. You must be warned that you will never get that time and that chance back.

Believe in yourself and all the dreams that you have. Having dreams and ambitions are great, but you have to follow those dreams with time and effort before those dreams become your true reality.

Believing in yourself does not mean be stuck up or conceited, it means it's ok to tell yourself "good job," for finishing a project. Believing in yourself also means allowing yourself to be proud of the things you do, whether it be for doing your homework, something that you did in a sports game, or something that you made or built. There are times that you need to pat yourself on the back and tell yourself good job. This is my version of believing in yourself.

"WARNING!" There are some things you need to know about "believing in yourself" because just believing in yourself, does not mean others will believe in you.

You may have ideas on what you want to do for a project or job, but others around you may not believe in what you want to do or how you want to do it. It is at times like this in life that you need to draw on your experience and knowledge to decide if it is time to take a stand. That's the meaning of believing in your self. There are times that you must to take a stand, be confident in yourself, but don't be over confident. None of us knows everything and we all have room for improvement in one area or another. You can believe in yourself and the things you do without having an attitude or being cocky. I strive

to be humble as I believe in myself.
****

As teenagers, one of the most important things that you will have to learn in life is that there are things that you can do that can't be undone.

SUICIDE CAN'T BE UNDONE!!!

This is something that needs to be burned into your memory so that its automatic like not pissing in your pants as if they were diapers. You automatically look to find a bathroom when you need to pee, "right"? So, there are many other things that you need to learn to do automatically in order to help take the confusion out of your life and give you clarity. The younger that you are when you learn this, the more prepared you will be to handle situations in life that test you -- situations like your friends doing drugs, having sex or drinking. You have your own mind and you should always be your own person. I know the temptation to go along with the crowd and there were times as a teenager that I went along with the crowd, which is what weak people do.

Going along with the group is when you change from being an individual person to being a sheep. Going along with the crowd is fine when you are at a ballgame routing for the home team, but your life is not a game. When your friends are doing drugs or having sex before they should, then going along with the crowd is not the wisest move that you could make. It is your choice in life; you can be the "sheep herder," and "you" call all the shots in your life or you can be a "sheep," not having your own mind or ability to make your own decisions.

I stress to you that it is much better to be the sheep herder than the sheep because sheep eventually get led slaughter.

All people in this world learn from the experiences of others, good or bad, right or wrong, we all learn from each other. Whether you learn from your mother and father, brothers or sisters, or from teachers, professors, mentors, your friends, books, DVD's, TV, or newspapers;

you need to learn to get the knowledge that will take you through a successful life. There is no age limit to this learning. There are only the limitations that you put on yourself. You should be as open to learning when you are 60 years old as when you're 16 years old. These things you learn along the way are all tools for you to use.

Example:

"Don't drink and drive!"

Four simple words that can save your life or someone else's. I know five people who have either driven drunk and died or got hit by a drunk driver. Don't drink or do drugs when you drive. This should be so automatic in your head that you don't even have to think about it "like breathing." This is what I mean by automatic.

As children and teenagers, we are not born with all the answers. As a matter of fact, all we do know is how to suck on a nipple and pee, everything else has to be learned; so, don't be afraid to ask questions.

Not knowing something will not get you into trouble most of the time. Saying you know something or you can do something and you really can't, this "WILL" get you into trouble, time and time again.

Most of these tools are simple, but with a clouded mind even the simplest things can become complicated. This book is meant to help you find clarity both as a teenager and as an adult. I hope you can have an open mind to allow yourself to take in these insights from my experiences, both the good ones and the bad.

I know that it's hard for troubled teenagers to take advice into your heart and into your head; advice from parents, teachers or books like this one. Teenagers don't have a problem getting advice from their friends, though, as if their friends have some more credibility than their parents or teachers. If friends that you are asking advice from are the same age as you, they probably don't know much more than you, do they?

You need to accept a basic fact, that "OLDER PEOPLE," also usually known as adults, have more knowledge and wisdom due to age. Accepting that what they're telling you comes from a lifetime of trail and error would be a wise thing to do on your part. It's the old cliché that "teenagers think they know it all." Hell, when I was 16, 17, or 18, I thought that I knew it all and so did your parents. So, parents remember this as you deal with them. They think that since we're older, we must be out of the loop and over the hill. We have no grasp of what they're feeling. I hope the teenagers who read this will realize that we are all just trying to help them become better people. Being a good son or daughter, or a good friend is not automatic, it is taught and learned just like everything else in our lives. Being cocky and fool hearty is part of being a teenager. Rebelling against your parents is part of it too, but this is just part of growing up and we all grow up sooner or later. Hopefully, with the right guidance and tools, you will grow up sooner.

Teenagers, you need to allow yourself to be taught and most of what you will be taught will be from your parents, teachers and other mentors. If you haven't heard the old expression "If I only new then, what I know now"... Well you've heard it now. I heard this a lot when I was growing up. I heard it from parents and teachers and there is nothing that is truer. This wisdom comes with age, there is no other way to get it. It is this wisdom that you need to take in. You need to know that there is no shame in not knowing everything as a teenager. No one ever does at 15, 16, or 17. I was taught by my mentor, Jethro. We worked together for 14 years. He was the drummer for many bands and I was his drum technician. In the many years we worked together he taught me thousands of things. I think the most valuable thing that he taught was to learn and be able to do as much as you can in life. He also taught me how to be humble and honorable with your friends and in your work. This advice alone has helped me in my life immeasurably. I hope from my soul that the advice in this book will help you through the teenage years, help you be a better parent and help you be a better family.

Teenagers, you have all the power that you need to succeed in this world. Don't give up your power to suicide. Don't let your temporary problem or issue control you, your thoughts or your actions. You need to be in control of your life and actions at all times. I know this is not easy, but it is possible. Life and living should not be taken for granted. I think you owe it to the miracle of life and to God to persevere and do your best at everything you do. Suicide is the wrong answer to your problem.

I beg you to do whatever it takes to get through the day and live. Live for yourself as well as for those whose lives you touch, like your family and friends. Please know this fact and keep it in your mind; suicide does not only end your life, but it hurts all the people who love you.

In this country, as well as in most countries, we use expressions to get certain points across to those whom we interact with throughout our lives. This book has some of those expressions in it like the following two:

"HINDSIGHT IS 20/20" AND "MONDAY MORNING QUARTER BACK".

Hindsight is 20/20 means: To look at something after it has already happened and pick apart what you did or did not do to come up with ideas of what you should or should not have done instead. To look at something after the fact. The expression "Monday morning quarter back" comes from watching Sunday football games and then discussing them on Monday. Doing the same thing, discussing them after the fact and suggesting what they should or shouldn't have done differently in the game. They mean the same thing.

I tell you this as a fact, hindsight is 20/20 and you have this hindsight with everything you will do in your life except one thing, "SUICIDE."

You can look back at your math or English test and you can look back on your basketball game or your dance recital. You can also look back on all your good and bad dates, toss around what you should or shouldn't have done differently.

You cannot look back after suicide!

There is no looking back to see what you could have done differently because

"SUICIDE IS PERMANENT!"

Most of the time, this expression is used after something bad has happened. You'll hear, well, "hindsight is 20/20." In this book, I'm looking at and getting over my past demons. I'm praying that I can get you to find a reason to kick your problems in the ass and continue moving forward in your life if it takes a day, a week, months or even years. In my case, it did take years and, if I could do it, so can you. This is your life, don't give it up to suicide.

Your life is what I'm talking about; your life is precious and is the only life you have; so, please, "DON"T WASTE IT." I'm not trying to preach to you, but I am telling you in plain black and white that I know exactly how you feel. I know with the right people around you and the right advice, you can get past the thought of suicide as an answer.

My advice to parents about hindsight is as follows: Don't be thinking of what you could have done differently as you stand at your child's funeral. Yes, I said your child's funeral. There are 28 parents a day doing this as the statistics show, so, please be an attentive parent, look for the warning signs of a troubled teen and take immediate action to help them. This is your responsibility as a parent.

We depend upon our parents, first and foremost, for teaching, guidance and inspiration to nurture us through the beginning of our lives. In our mid- and late- teens we need to take what we've learned so far and add that to our inner inspirations to take us farther forward in whatever direction we may go in our lives.

If you are born to a parent or parents who have no inspiration, this does not mean that you can't find inspiration, or inspiration can't find you.

One day you could be doing something and out of the clear blue sky you see something on TV that you've never seen before and it catches your eye or you might hear something on the radio or read in a magazine, something that makes you stop and look to see what it is. With this one look by chance, you could get the inspiration to do what ever it is that will make your life's desires full and complete. It's all around you, "INSPIRATION," that is. You just have to be open minded enough to let it in. Inspiration can come from your friends or other family members. You will find it in teachers from your school, books you read, music you listen to and in the places you go in your life.

Inspiration does not have to be in the spoken word. Some of the greatest achievements in life have come from the things that we see with our own eyes, such as man looking at the moon and watching the birds fly. With inspiration from these visions, man now flies and has walked on the moon. Nature is my biggest inspiration. To me, there is no other place I'd rather be than in a boat, on a lake surrounded by trees looking up into a clear blue sky from sunrise to sunset fishing, listening to the birds and the wind in the trees. If there could be perfection in life this would be it for me.

We all need to strive for our own perfection in life. A life of happiness and peace, this is perfection in my eyes and what I wish for those who read this book.

Life is wind which blows in many directions that will never have a chance with "SUICIDE!!!"

No matter how bad life may seem, suicide is no answer. I can tell you this from my own experience of failures and successes. I'm 22 years from the point in my life when I attempted suicide. Twenty-two years that I would have never seen or experienced, if my best friends had not stopped me from ending my life. Twenty-two years of working hard and shedding my blood, sweat and tears. Twenty-two years of the most incredible memories of being with my best friends on the tops of 10,000 foot mountains in the snow or being in the middle of the desert riding dirt bikes and having a camp fire 10 feet high.

I'm grateful and I thank God for every day that I live on. I wouldn't trade these years for anything now that I'm looking forward to the next twenty years and the twenty years after that. My friends actually grabbed me by the shoulders and shook me, screaming at me, telling me that they didn't want me to kill myself. This is the reason that I'm alive today and I'm now trying to shake you both, teenagers and parents. I believe that with the right tools you can get through a rough time in life without suicide as an option. I pray this book is a good tool for you in life. I'm begging you to reach down inside yourself, live through today and get to tomorrow, any way that you can. Talk to your family, friends, teachers, counselors or religious scholars and know that there is help out there. Again, I repeat that there is no shame in learning things you don't know.

There is no shame in asking questions or in asking for help.

I know what it's like to want to crawl into a hole and die over and over, day after day, year after year. I'm here to say that you can overcome this feeling as I have overcome it.

I found inspiration to make that feeling disappear; I found inspiration in my friends and in music, as well as, in the mountains, on the ocean and in the sky. Inspiration is different for everyone. With my words, I hope that I've shared with you inspiration to live long, to understand how precious life is and the realization that you only are given one life.

DO NOT COMMIT SUICIDE. SUICIDE IS NOT AN ANSWER TO ANYTHING!!!

Now, as a 38 year old man who attempted suicide at ages 16 and 18,

I thank God everyday for my friends and for being alive. I've written this book to keep you alive till you're 38, 48, or 98. I promise you that at all of these ages you will be thankful that you are alive and love your years and years of great memories, just as I am.

****

I know as a child and a teenager, things are engrained in you that last years, sometimes a lifetime. Something someone like a parent or a bully at school does to try and bring you down.

I understand this all too well because my mother did this to me from the age of eight years old when she told me that she didn't like my friends and that I should be friends with the kids she liked. Looking back it just makes me want to puke. I was eight years old and hanging out with the wrong crowd in her eyes.

I did what all kids do in grade school. I gravitated toward kids with similar interests and personalities. As I got older, in my teens, my mother's dislike for my friends only grew. My friends were something I battled about with my mother during my entire childhood. My mother constantly told me that she wished I was different and that I should be like the other kids, with whom she wanted me to be friends. Even as a grown man of 37 years old, she told me that she wished I was different.

That was the straw that broke the camel's back; it was at that moment I decided to keep her out of my life.

It is hard to overcome negative things told to you by one or both of your parents. This is what I mean by engrained; the shit that you hear day in and day out meant to belittle you. Whomever it is coming from, all that matters is that you don't take it in.

"DON'T TAKE IT IN"

Stand tall and be strong in your life always. We all have the power not to take any of this in. That's right; you have the power, whether you're 7 to 9, or 15 to 17, the power is there.

It is your inner strength, know you have it, use it to let the negative stuff bounce right off of you. I do know that as a child or teenager you feel that you're stuck in a situation you can't control. I beg you "to give you back control of your life".

DON'T GIVE UP YOUR CONTROL TO SUICIDE!!!

Suicide is no answer to your temporary problems.
****

STRIVING FOR APPROVAL…

When we are young or as we get older, this is something we all do. It is natural, whether it's from our parents or from our friends, it's just something that we do. I sought approval from my mother my entire life until last year. I know now that I will never get her approval and I've finally "ACCEPTED" that fact. I do know exactly what its like and that I want approval on the things I do, such as pottery or the waterfalls that I make and this book. I want to hear that people like what I've made with my own two hands. The bottom line is that I have to be pleased in what I do just as you need to be pleased with that which you choose to put in your heart and soul.

You shouldn't live your life solely looking for the approval of others. You need to approve of yourself, live for yourself, not for the satisfaction of others. When you are confident in yourself and the things you do, your family and friends will, more than likely, give you the approval you seek to find within yourself.

Approval or non-approval from your family or friends shouldn't make or break who you are and you shouldn't live your life for people who are negative and evil toward you. There may be people in your life who constantly find fault with you, no matter what you do. They are always negative toward you and the things you do, whether they are friends or family, you need to get them out of your life, for your own peace of mind.

That's right, I said get them "OUT of your LIFE." There is no rule or law that says you have to keep them in your life, especially if they are generally mean, evil, bad people. This is a big part of life, picking out the good people from the bad. I've found as I go through my life, there are people who it seems will go out of their way to lie, mislead and deceive you right to your face. I call them the bad people.

I've also found out, (the hard way I might add), some of these people who do these bad things to you, come with titles. Titles such as mother, father, brother, sister, and the people you thought were your friends. It's sad but true; some parents are mean, cruel and evil. The problem is you can't really get away from that kind of situation until you are 18 years old. If this is the case, you must gravitate towards teachers, coaches, councilors, and parents of your friends for support.

As for your cruel friends, I say get rid of them instantly. There are a lot of people in this world. I believe with some effort on your part, you will find friends who are trustworthy and good at heart and I also believe that if you put out a good "VIBE," a good vibe will come back to you.

BE IN CONTROL OF YOUR LIFE, DON'T LET LIFE CONTROL YOU.

Teenagers, you shouldn't be in such a rush to grow up. This is the only time in life you'll be a teenager, SO ENJOY IT!!! Revel in it!!! You will not get another chance and you will regret it if you don't live your childhood to the fullest extent.

Some of the best times I have right now are when I look back on the things I did with my friends. The same friends I've had for 30 years: Jamie, Dino, Mike, Rafe and Jethro. There is no price that you can put on life long friendships like these. These guys are more than friends to me, they are my family till the day I die. These guys kept me looking toward a future. They kept me from suicide at a point in my life when all I wanted to do was DIE. I love them with all my heart and soul. Thanks guys!!!

I hope these things are helpful and give you some peace of mind. I want to give you a point of view from someone who has been in your shoes. I remember exactly what it was like to be a pissed off teenager. This book can help you, but you also need to help yourself. You can do this by learning and using tools you need to be in control of your life. You don't have to be a pissed off teenager.

I know everyone's individual situation is different as far as the reason why you feel you need to take your own life as an answer to your problems. Please, dig down deep inside yourself and find the strength to overcome any problem or any hurdle that stands in your way. I plead again to you,

"DON'T TAKE YOUR LIFE OVER A TEMPORARY PROBLEM"!!!

I promise you that in time these problems will pass.

There are times when you have to sit back, relax and look at what your problems are, one at a time. You need to accept that life has problems that come up from time to time. You get stronger as you take them on and overcome them. If you can't find an answer or a solution to your problem, then go outside of yourself and ask questions. Knowledge is power and you obtain both knowledge and power by asking questions and finding answers.

It can be a waste of effort and time to try to take on many things at once. You will find out that if you try to do too much at once, you can actually end up not accomplishing anything at all.

Taking on too much will become a big problem in itself. If you see yourself "taking on too much," then you need to "SLOW DOWN"!!! There is nothing written in stone that says you have to do a hundred things at once. Slow down, breathe deeply and take care of things one at a time. Putting your time and effort into things this way allows you to focus your concentration to one task from beginning to completion.

I recommend that you do this for a couple of reasons: First, to just simplify your day-to-day life. The second is that you will find that you accomplish more and this is major to finish what you started. You will have obstacles and problems both big and small, not just as a teenager, but throughout your life. Problems with your parents, school, friends or teachers, boy or girlfriends, or a problem just with yourself. There are times all of us have been depressed due to the stresses in life.

A body builder gets bigger and stronger the more he works out. It is the same with problems that come your way. The more you take them on "one at a time," you will get stronger as you overcome them.

"OVERCOME YOUR PROBLEMS"

Get stronger for today, tomorrow and every day for the rest of your long life.

"SUICIDE IS NOT AN ANSWER TO YOUR PROBLEMS. IT IS THE END OF YOUR LIFE"!!!

Take your time and do whatever it takes to understand and overcome your problems. I beg you to listen to me because I almost killed myself and I did not see an end to my problems because I didn't get the help I needed from my mother. Twenty-two years later I'm here to tell the story of my life in order to let you teenagers know that I know exactly how you feel and I want to help you find a way to "UNDERSTAND AND OVERCOME" anything that blocks your path on the journey of life.

Again, I urge you to ask questions. You can ask your parents, your teachers or friends, or there are counselors, priests and clergy. There are groups who meet to discuss every different topic there is from drugs and alcohol, to relationships, youth groups and everything in between. These people live for you to come and ask questions, so go check it out. If you're having a hard time talking to your parents or friends, you need to understand that if you need help, it's out there and you have to seek it out.

IF YOU NEED HELP...SEEK IT! YOU ARE WORTHY OF IT!!!

You can't expect people to know and be waiting for the moment you need help because this may not exist.

Here are some helpful ways to understand and overcome any problem:

Write things down on paper, like a journal or maybe in poems or songs.

Sometimes when you write things down and read them back to yourself, you get a clearer vision of what you are thinking about.

Writing down your thoughts, both good and bad can be a powerful thing.

Remember not to limit yourself as you do this, you don't have to just write about the problems and pains. You should also write down your dreams of what you'd like to do with your life and the places you'd like to go in this world -- all your aspirations. This is an important tool that will bring you a freedom and peace you can't get any other way.

Another thing that can be powerful is drawing or painting. Sometimes I don't have anything to say, but yet I want to get both the good and bad feelings inside of me out. When I feel like this, I draw and sketch in a book and when I look back at the pictures over time, they take me back to how I was feeling at that time in my life. I always date the pictures and the words I write so when I look at them 20 and 30 years later I know when I did them.

****

ESCAPING THE BLACK HOLE......

I'm going to start this section with saying "DON'T BE A VICTIM"!!!

Don't be a pre-teen victim, a teenage victim or a victim anytime in your life. Don't be a victim to your parents, your friends, your teachers or anybody else that belittles you and puts you down. They do this from a deep hole in their soul that they cannot fulfill. They do this because they themselves feel insufficient. People with no self worth will always try to bring down others to their level. These are people with no goodness and no happiness in their lives.

These people can never bring you down, if you don't let them.

You need to be firm and always stand tall. Starting from as young as possible to the end of your life, be confident and believe in yourself.

Don't be a victim to yourself, "SUICIDE IS NO SOLUTION" and it is making yourself a victim!!!

I hope I'm not the only one who is asking and begging you to hear that you can get beyond this moment in life. But if I am, then so be it. I'm letting you know that there's more out there than just SUICIDE as an answer. I know this from experience. I tried to kill myself 2 times as a teenager and when I was a teenager, I wanted to die every day from 13 until I was 17.

At these ages death and suicide should have been the farthest things from my mind, but they weren't. I attempted suicide during these years for one reason, I hated my mother and wanted to get back at her by committing suicide. I thought by committing suicide that she would feel my pain. I wrote suicide notes telling her that I did this because of her and the way she treated me compared to my sister. I wanted her to live every day of the rest of her life knowing that her son killed himself directly because of her actions.

I was almost a victim of my mother.

I'm begging you not to be a victim to anyone!!! I know what it's like to want to shove all your pain in the face of the one who's bringing you pain. Don't allow yourself to be a victim, use your inner strength and overcome all the hurdles in your life.

I understand the black hole, a place that has no control.

No control except for suicide may wrongly be the only escape that you see. I wanted to escape with suicide. I've felt that pain. I've felt your pain and I want you to know that you're not alone.
YOU ARE NOT ALONE!!!

I'm 38 and it took me a long time to realize that suicide is no escape and no answer to my problems. I found this out thanks to the love of my friends. I pray that when you read this you come to the same conclusion.

SUICIDE IS NO ANSWER…JUST THE END OF YOUR LIFE!

There is a thing called self-mutilation and it can take two forms; one is physical, and the other is emotional.

I know first hand about both of these, but it is the emotional self-mutilation that I put myself through that is the hardest pattern to break. I also understand how teenagers get driven to this point by believing what others say when they are trying to tear them down. Teenagers hear certain things repeatedly and it gets to the point where they don't have to hear it any more because they start to say it to themselves. This is when emotional self-mutilation starts in a teenager's life and I want to help avoid this.

I know that feeling of standing still, yet your insides are spinning like a tornado. You can't fall, you can't jump, there is no movement, you are just frozen in time with not even enough energy to breathe.

There is no calm in the eye of the storm…it's all storm. From sun up to sun down living in the storm.

Suicide is not the umbrella to save you from this storm.

I fully understand how it feels to be backed into a corner. The walls close in and the feeling of being trapped takes over your mind, body and soul. Trapped by your parents and trapped by feelings of worthlessness, pain, anger and uncontrollable frustration. I understand how these feelings and problems can get out of control, but I also understand that control can be regained.

There are different things that I did at different times through out my life to regain control and extinguish the thoughts of suicide.

There were times when I just simply just ran to the point of exhaustion. Sometimes I got on my bike and just pedaled as fast as I could for as long as I could, not ever wanting to look back. Then there were times that I just shut the door of my room and turned up my music as loud as it would go, screaming my ass off to every song.

In the midst of emotional frustration and devastation, it helps me to clear my head when I physically exhaust myself by running or singing loudly.

Suicide is not opening up a door to safety, it's closing the door on life.

I'm pleading with you to dig down, find the strength that's in your soul and stay alive.

They say that the only things in life that are guaranteed are death and taxes. Well I'm changing that right now. I'm giving you this "GUARANTEE" and I will believe this until the day I die:

When you are 5 or even 40 years farther down the road, from the time you wanted to take your life, looking back on the memories of your life, I guarantee you will be happy to the umpteenth degree that you did not commit suicide. This is my guarantee to you.

****

BREATHE   DEEP!!!!

"BREATHING" is something that can make you feel better.

Simply Breathe deep ,breathe slow and relax. I've found that when I was in the heat of my anger and fighting with my mother, ten to thirty minutes have gone by and I get light headed because I haven't taken a breath. I finally got to the point that I wanted to stop breathing forever.

Black skies, black walls and the black hole, I was a teenager that could never see a happy tomorrow.

Being a teenager is a small part of your life in actual time, if you figure a lifetime of 60 to 80 years. Hear me and comprehend that being a teenager is a relatively small, nine year period of your life.

Being a teenager is a great thing, but the reality is that there is more to life than just being a teenager. I know teenagers feel like they will be teenagers forever. The truth is that you will grow up faster than you know and this book is meant to help you get through the difficult and frustrating times of being a teenager.

Looking back on being a teenager will always bring a smile to your face. Even the most turbulent years of your youth will bring a smile to your face. This is because these years are over and you now run your own life. The thing you will remember first will be the good times you did have with your friends and family. This is also a guarantee that I will believe forever. You will also remember the turbulent and bad times, but they will not have much importance anymore and you will smile because you are alive.

I know in my heart of hearts that a young person from 11 to 20 years of age does not want to commit suicide. I know this deep down in my bones.

Suicide is 99.9% of the time a cry out for help and attention, in my opinion. This was my extreme cry out for attention. I was trying to get my mother's attention and revenge at the same time. The revenge was the suicide notes I left for her.

I thought my Mother would change after I attempted suicide and I thought I'd get her attention. I was wrong!!! It has taken me over twenty years to realize that she will never change and you can't change people.

Suicide only changes you from alive to dead, that's it.

The problem has not changed and suicide is no solution.

I'm begging you to live through today and on to tomorrow because life is like wine and it gets better with age. You need to do what it takes to overcome the thoughts of suicide and gain wisdom with age.

Don't be a victim of intimidation. I understand that as a young child or as a teenager, it's easy to be intimidated.

Intimidated by your parents, your teachers and your friends, I know how this feels and you are not alone in this feeling either. You need know that you have the power inside you to overcome this feeling of intimidation.

Not only can you overcome this feeling but you can turn it around 180 degrees and intimidate the person doing this to you. You do this by being strong in your soul with conviction in your heart. Don't be a push over and know that if you give in to the intimidation of someone, they will feel comfortable doing this to you over and over until you get strong enough to stop it.

First, you need to understand that anyone who tries to purposely intimidate you is a weak person.

That's right I said "WEAK" and if someone tries to intimidate you to get what they want, it's because they are seeking power over you.

This happens because they are weak people on their own, so they try to intimidate others to show that they are not weak. I want all teenagers to know that you have the power inside of you, the power to never let anyone intimidate you.

Dig down, find the strength that's in your soul and stand tall in the face of those who might try to tear you down with intimidation.

I was intimidated from a young age by my mother. Having a mother that started telling me when I was in second grade that I should be more like this kid instead of that kid because in her eyes I was not good enough as I was.

The way my Mother intimidated me at such a young age made me feel like it was a personal attack. I also had teachers who did their best to intimidate me because I acted and dressed differently than other kids. This posed some kind of threat to them. I learned over time that the only way to overcome this intimidation from others was to stand strong, look it in the face and not back down.

I want you to know that it's all right to be yourself even if you don't get the approval other others.

As a teenager there will be hundreds of situations that come your way where you may feel intimidated by your family, friends, teachers and especially as you start to work, your bosses may try to intimidate you.
When this happens to you, (sooner or later it will), you will need to recognize it for what it is, stand strong and stop it dead in it's tracks.

"YOU CANNOT BE INTIMIDATED IF YOU DO NOT ALLOW IT TO HAPPEN!!!"

Peer pressure from your friends can be one of the worst kinds of intimidation. You may have friends who are experimenting with drugs, sex, or they may lie to their parents and they want you to lie to your parents, too. The intimidation may be something small or go to the extreme. Whatever it is, you have the power to overcome any intimidation. No one can overcome this feeling of intimidation for you. You do it in your heart and in your soul by being strong in your convictions. This is a powerful thing and you own it,

"CONVICTION"

Don't be a follower in your life, be a leader. A leader does not get people to follow them by intimidation; but rather, by inspiration.

A leader inspires people by being strong with truth and conviction. You need to strive to be a leader in your life.

****

THE CONSEQUENCES OF SUICIDE:

I fully understand the consequences of suicide thanks to the ones who truly love me. I want teenagers and anyone who feels that suicide is your only option to fully understand the consequences of this action.

I believe that suicide is done with vengeance towards the one or ones who have brought you to this point of wanting to take your own life. I know you want to hurt the person or people who, at this point in your life, are giving you grief. I understand this thinking,

Suicide is not the way to overcome this grief in your life.

The best way to overcome this grief and pain is to rise above the person or people who are bringing you down.
The consequences of this vengeance towards the ones you want to hurt are usually minor.

Whether you're trying to hurt your mother, father or the kids that pick on you at school, your suicide will not effect them in the manor that you hope it will.

The major consequences are to the ones who truly love you like your family, friends and the people you've touched in your life.

These are the people that you will truly crush by committing suicide.
Grandparents, aunts, uncles, your best friends, teachers and all the people who you spend time with will all be devastated for a wide array of reasons if you take your life.

If you are of the mind that no one will care if you take your life, I say to you "BULLSHIT."

There are lots of people in your life who love you and want to see you grow up and do well in life. It's just your mind and your vision that are clouded because you are frustrated. You don't see a clear way out of the black hole that you're in right now.

You need to dig down and use your inner strength to overcome this vengeance towards the people who you perceive are trying to bring you down.

The best vengeance you can do to these people is to show them that you are not too weak to overcome the things they try to do to you.

Overcome these people first by getting them out of your life.

If there are people in your life who are hurting you in one way or another then get them out of your life. You have no obligation to these people at all and this you need to understand and comprehend. Don't let evil people bring you down, whoever they may be. Life is precious, don't give up your life to vengeance.

****

I'd like to talk to you now about thinking and preparing for your future. Here are some more facts:

You need "MONEY" for everything, that's right, everything!!!

If you want a apartment or home to live in, you need money. If you want to eat food or have a car, you need money. Do you see where I'm going here? You'll have to have money to do any of the things you probably enjoy doing like travel, buying new clothes, new CD's or a car. This list goes on forever...

If you are the 1% who are independently wealthy from birth, then I guess you can just sit back and laugh through this section. As for everyone else, you will need to find something to do that adults call, "making a living."

This is just one more thing in life that you need to learn, accept, and go on. So accept that you will, at some point, have to make a living for yourself and that may include a wife or husband, and maybe even children someday.

How's that for a scary thought?

Take a look at how your parents provide you with a roof over your head and food on your table. My guess is that most of you have clothes and shoes that your parents have provided for you by " making a living."

Ask your parents questions about how they make a living, if you don't know what they do for work. Ask them if they like their job or career and what they dreamed about being when they were kids. If they're not doing what they dreamed about when they were kids, ask them why not? Ask them if they are happy doing what they do and why?

Ask them about the hard work it takes to support a family. The point here is to not take for granted that you know the answers to these questions.

As far as you making a living for yourself and your future family, here are 3 ways I see that you can do this and these are my definitions:

1) A "job" is something that one does for money. This is something that you do with no love or passion, you just do it, like a robot. It does not matter what it is that you're doing, if you hate it, "it's a job." Something you do day in and day out like a machine with no on or off switch. Know that what I have just described is what most people of working age across the world do. Yes, most people across the entire world hate their jobs.

I've come to this conclusion from speaking with hundreds of people, in which about 95% of them hate their jobs.

My advice to you is: don't make a living by having a job unless you have no other choice!!!

2) The second way to make a living is to have a career. I'm sure that you've heard of this "career" thing. Now don't get me wrong, I think a career is a good thing, if you have a career that you love and wouldn't want to do anything else. It has been my observation that there are many people who spent years in college or trade schools to get into a career that they just ended up hating.

Having a career that you hate takes you nowhere in life. To me, it's almost the same as having a job, "IT SUCKS"…

3) The third way and the way I suggest is to "MAKE A LIVING DOING WHAT YOU LOVE TO DO"!!!

This is possible for anyone who lives in a free country. Thank God for the U.S.A.

Make a living doing what you love to do. How can you do this? No matter what age you are now, I'm sure there are things that you like to do. Start there. Take a look at your interests, whether you are into science, sports, music, art, politics, movies, cars & motorcycles, traveling, different languages, cooking, animals or whatever you like to spend your time doing. There are these and hundreds of other things that you should think about as a way to make a living.

What you need to know at an early age is that you will spend most of your life doing whatever it is you choose to make a living.

This is called "WORK" and work "DOES NOT" seem like work if you are doing something that you love to do.

You actually want to "GO TO WORK" when you do what you love to do for a living. This is a fact!!! The work that you do to make the money that you will live on for the rest of your life does not have to be something you hate.

Hear me on this fact, PLEASE!!! When you do what you love for a living, hours go by like minutes. You're not always looking at the clock to see when it's lunchtime, or when it's time to go home. This means that if you love to paint or draw, get a job where you paint and draw all day long. If you love music, then get a job as a D.J. at a radio station and play music all day long. If you want to save lives, then become a doctor or paramedic.

I hope you are getting the point I'm making here. You need to take a good look at yourself and what you want to do with your life.

Don't feel like you are locked into one thing or another. As you get older, you will always find new interests and some of your old interests may fade away. If you have done one career for a number of years and you want to change to a different career, then you need to do that.

Don't waste your life not living up to your full potential. If you do, you are just slowly killing yourself in a life that's moving to fast as it is. Do what you love for a living is my suggestion.

I'm going to give you some ideas now on how you can work doing what you love for a living and/or working in an industry that deals with the things you love. This list may go a little over the top, but I wish I had someone who would have told me what I am telling you now, as a teenager. These are some examples of doing what you love for a living:

If you love music than here is a list of things you can do in the field of music. If you want to play music for a living than start by taking lessons in : singing, guitar, drums, piano, flute, trumpet, violin or any other instrument you can think of. Take lessons and practice, practice, practice.

If you feel that you might not have the talent to be a professional musician, don't let this stop you from being in the field of music.

There are many more things that you can do in this field without being a musician.

If you are more business oriented then you could be a band manager or agent. There isn't a band going that doesn't have a manager to take care of all that has to be done in the way of booking shows and studio time. Maybe you have great hearing, this is the job of a sound man. If you are a sound man for live shows, it is your job to bring the music that is being played on stage to the audience via the sound system. This is one of the most important jobs that one can do for any band, whether it's rock and roll, country, rap, jazz or R&B music.

There are people who only write songs for bands and singers. So, if you write poetry or songs, then this is something you should definitely look into. Maybe you like to take pictures, you could get a job with a music magazine and be paid to go on tour with bands and photograph bands in concert and behind the scenes. If you are big and strong, you could be a band's bodyguard or a roadie. Roadies are the people who set up all the band's instruments on stage or in the studio. If you want to be a lawyer and you love music, you could be a music lawyer. That's right, there are lawyers who only deal with bands and all the legalese of contracts with record company's and copyright laws.

If you love animals, there are lots of things you could do to make a living.

You could be a veterinarian. A good vet saves the lives of animals every week. Let me tell you that when you save a family's pet, you will forever be in their prayers.

If you don't want to be cooped up in a office all day looking at the same four walls, then let me suggest to you the possibility of being a large animal veterinarian. Large animal vet's spend their days going to ranches, working on horses, cows, goats and a variety of animals that are too big to be put in a car and taken to an office.

There are also vet's who work at every zoo in the country. You could work with animals like tigers, elephants, bears, camels, birds and this list goes on and on. You could become a pet trainer who trains animals for movies or pet shows.

There are magazines that are just about animals in which you could write about rodeos or take pictures for these magazines.

If you like cutting hair, you could be a dog groomer.
You could also train dogs to help blind people or to be a police dog. You could work on a ranch with horses and cattle or even be a lion tamer in the circus. There are wild animal parks and places such as Sea World where you can work with all kinds of different animals. Just imagine that you can get paid to swim with dolphins every day.

Don't let anything hold you back from doing what you love.

Maybe you want to change the world although it may sound far-fetched, you can change the world if you'd like to by being a scientist. A scientist can change the world by inventing things like a cure to diseases such as AIDS, Cancer, Heart Disease, Blindness. This list goes on and on.

You could also change the world by inventing a way to grow food in areas of the world where people have a hard time growing food.

You may have heard about two men who were named the Wright brothers. These two brothers had the dreams and desires to fly; so, with a lot of time, effort, trial and error, they built the first airplane.

You might be able to work at N.A.S.A. and help build rocket ships that take people to other planets.

Don't ever let anybody say that you can't do whatever it is in your heart and in your dreams.

How about being a doctor, like the doctor who did the first heart transplant. Just imagine being the doctor who first did what seemed like the impossible. Take a bad heart out of one person and put in a good heart from another person. This is what I mean about changing the world…pretty intense, yeah.

You could be a doctor who invents a procedure that saves lives all over the world, that's no little thing. You could be a plastic surgeon who works on burn victims or people who are disfigured from traumatic accidents.

If you'd like to work with children, then you can be come a pediatric doctor. Don't forget about the jobs that interact with other jobs. You may want to be a doctor, but you don't want the typical doctor job in a hospital or in an office and you also like sports. You could be a sports medicine doctor who works for football, baseball or basketball teams, etc…

There are also individual sports like tennis, golf or swimming.

Don't put any limitations on yourself or you will regret it in the long run.

Maybe you like to take care of people. You could do this and get paid for doing it by being a nurse. I'll tell you from experience that when you are lying in a hospital bedroom, there is no greater comfort than having a good nurse to help you.

Again I say to you that you need to do what you love for a living.

There are jobs like fireman or policeman. Both of these jobs have an element of danger and risk, but there can be incredible satisfaction too. You might be the first one to go inside a burning building and save someone's life. Or you could be a detective who discovers that one clue that solves a crime and helps put a violent criminal in jail.

Maybe you want to be a lawyer or a judge helping to keep criminals off the streets. You may want to change the world by being a mayor, governor, senator, or even the President of the United States of America.

If you are into cars, trucks or motorcycles, then there are hundreds of jobs you could do to be involved in the car or motorcycle industry. It's all up to you and your desires. You could be a race car driver or race motorcycles. If you don't have the skills to be a race car driver, but you want to work with races cars then you need to look into being a mechanic or one of the other many jobs that are working with the race teams. You might have incredible engineering skills, you could design cars or motorcycles for the future. If you like to deal with people, there are jobs in promotions, sales and advertising all dealing with cars and motorcycles. If you like to drive, there are some people who only drive around in the newest cars testing them out before they're sold to the general public. Maybe you'd like to get paid to crash cars, that's right get paid a lot of money to crash cars, trucks, and motorcycles. You can do this by becoming a stunt man or woman.

If you like to take pictures or if you like to use video cameras, then there's lots of different things you could do in this field of work.

A photographer can bring the world to people who can't go out and see for themselves. Whether you photograph landscapes, animals, cities, wars, sporting advents, famous people or you name it, you could travel the world working for newspapers or magazines and get paid for bringing the world to people.

If you'd like to work as a video cameraman, you could work on making movies or at television studios. Every time you see a news report on TV and you see a reporter out on a location describing and showing you what's going on where they are, there is a camera man there standing right in front of them.

If you want to work with children, then I want to suggest to you the idea of being a teacher. There is nothing more needed in this world than good teachers. Some of the teachers I had through my years in school helped me not only with giving me an education, but they taught me things about life that you can't learn in books.

I also had football and baseball coaches who helped instill confidence in me through what they taught me. There is nothing better than having a good teacher and if want to be a teacher than I pray you are one of the best.

One of my good friends is a fishing boat captain. He sails across the ocean and takes people fishing. If you like the water then there is nothing better than having a job where you are on the ocean, lakes or rivers all day. There are jobs you could get on cruise ships or freighters that take you across the seven seas.

There are jobs that interact with other jobs too. What I mean here is that you might want to be a police officer or a fireman, and you would like to work on a boat at the same time. Well there are jobs just like this. Harbor patrol are policemen who work in boats both on lakes and the ocean. In cities that have oceans or rivers around them, you can bet that there are fireboats that work in the harbors.

If you are creative then maybe you need to be an artist. Being an artist can cover a wide range of things. This could be someone who draws or paints pictures. There are hundreds of jobs that you can have where you get paid to draw or paint all day. You might want to be a cartoonist and draw for movies or magazines. You could be a sketch artist who sits in a courtroom sketching those on trial. There are jobs for graphic artists where you work for advertising and sales companies drawing and sketching ads for products in magazines and commercials that are seen worldwide.

Some artists work with material such as clay, marble, bronze and other materials that you sculpt from a lump of nothing into a beautiful work of art.

You might want to be an architect and design homes and office buildings. There are artists who make jewelry and design clothes for models and movies.

What I'd like to stress to you here is simple because if you are creative and have the desire to make something beautiful out of nothing, you need to be an artist.

I'm trying to show you that your options in life are unlimited. The only limitations you have are the ones that you put upon yourself.

Every job in life has it's pro's and con's. They all have their ups and downs. The important thing here is that if you have a job that you truly love doing, there are a lot less downs. The sooner you understand this as a fact, the sooner you can take control of your life. This is the main point I'm trying to make in this book, you have the power to control your life. Don't give up that control to suicide.

"When you do what you love for a living," this is a dream come true. As you grow up, I suggest that you ask different people all along the way and from all walks of life, if they love what they are doing for a living. Ask the plumber, mailman, lawyer, doctor, cook, maid, the woman at the market check out stand with the name tag that says she's been there since 1981, your teachers and councilors. This list can go on forever, so I'll stop here.

Ask questions, and don't be embarrassed if you don't understand what someone tells you. Ask them to clarify the answer so that you can understand more clearly. Remember that the more knowledge you have, the more well rounded and intelligent you will be and this will help you in both your personal life as well as your professional life.

Everything that I've put down in this book is meant to get your attention.
I want to get your attention and then give you information while I have your attention. I do this in the hope that you take to heart that suicide is not an answer to your problems.

With this in mind, I give you this list of things you need to do to rid your mind from suicide. I'm a big proponent of physical exertion to clear your mind, which means that you need to get off your ass and stop dwelling on the negative things in your life, go out and make something positive for your life. Whether you do team sports, individual sports or you get yourself a hobby that gets you up and out of the house, all that matters is that there are hundreds of activities you can immerse yourself in to help rid you from thoughts of suicide.

There are times that you will want to do things by yourself, and other times you might want the company of your friends or family. The point is that you need to see how much there is to live for in life.

In most communities there are organizations that help put together teams and leagues for all kind of sports and events that happen though out the community, such as baseball, softball, football, soccer, bowling, marathons, swim meets, fishing contests, girl and boy scouts, golf tournaments, live theater plays, etc…

I'm a firm believer in being a part of a team sport or sports when you are young, ages 7 to10 right through high school. There are things you will learn that you can't get any other way, such as camaraderie, teamwork and respect for others.

The emotions of winning, losing and responsibility to your teammates will create bonds that you will have the rest of your life.

Please, if your parents are the kind of parents that don't give you much or any encouragement to go out and try one or all of the things that interest you, then it's up to you to bring it to your parent's attention that you want to be on a team sport or you want to join a club. Don't let what you want to do go by because you don't have any encouragement from your parents.

Some parents will only encourage you if you participate in the things that they want you to do, whether you like it or not. Don't let this discourage you in the slightest. You will find encouragement and support with the people who are already doing these activities.

It is up to you to get the information you need to start being involved in the activity you wish to become a part of; so, don't let asking questions and doing some leg work on your own discourage you from following your dreams and desires.

If you need some ideas of possible things you could do or get involved with, something that gives you the desire to live on, day after day, then here you go:

Go outside and ride a bike or run around the block. You might need to run five blocks or five miles, which you could do by yourself and which could be your time to clear your head and get away from the rat race for a little while.

Or, if you'd like to have company while you go for a walk, jog, run, or a bike ride, then you need to take it upon yourself to go out and find a friend, neighbor, or school mate that likes to do this kind of thing. In doing this, you might find that you like the feeling you get from running and, if so, then you should look into getting on to your school's track team. If your school does not have a track team, then you should take it upon yourself to find others who would want to be on a track team and put a team together.

You might also want to look in your community for local city marathons for and in which you could train and participate. You do have to put in some effort to do the things that you desire and dream about, sometimes it will take more effort than other times and that is just a part of life.

If you don't like to run then you might need to jump in the ocean, a lake or a pool. Do some laps in a pool or learn to surf, dive, fish, jet ski, water ski, wake board, or drive a boat. There is nothing like the freedom you feel when you are in the ocean or a lake.

If you want to keep your feet on the ground then maybe you should try playing tennis, racquet ball, ping pong, golf Frisbee, volley ball, baseball, football, basketball, hockey, and soccer.

Understand that the only limitations that you have are the ones you put upon yourself. There are times that you won't be able to find a friend to throw a ball around with, so you need to take it upon yourself to go down to the park and shoot some hoops or hit a tennis ball against a wall.

DON'T EVER LET LAZINESS SET IN AND RULE YOUR LIFE.

If you want to move fast across the ground then you need to get yourself some wheels in the form of roller skates, skateboards, bicycles, scooters, motorcycles, go carts.

There are some things without wheels that you can also go fast doing. You could try ice skating, skiing or snowboarding. If you want to watch other people go fast, then you need to go to the races. Cars, trucks, motorcycles, boats, go carts, BMX, you name it, but if it has wheels then you can be sure that somewhere there are people racing it. If it doesn't have wheels, well people will race anything: there are horse, dog, frog, pig, camel, sheep, donkey, goat, and camel races. This is just the tip of the iceberg for things that will get you up and out of the house. Everybody has things that drive them, something that makes them feel alive.

As a teenager you need to look inside yourself and find what drives you and what makes you feel alive. Once you've know what that is, then go out and conquer that thing.

Not everything you do to clear your head has to be physical.
I believe that you can get the peace of mind you're looking for through reading books, listening to music or playing chess with a friend. Draw a picture, write a poem, watch a movie, bake a cake, talk on the phone to a friend or knit a quilt. I believe that these and other nonphysical activities will help you to relax, but there is just a different

type of feeling that you can get from physical exhaustion when trying to relieve stress from your life.

****

Even though I've written this book, I can't honestly say to you or to myself that there aren't times that I still don't want to crawl up in a hole and die. There are times that I feel worthless, whether it be in my own eyes or how I am perceived by other people.

Even though over time this feeling subsides quicker than it used to, I still struggle. Experience has taught me to hang tough, persevere and believe that there is a reason for every hardship that comes my way.

This is the one of the main points that I want teenagers to get from reading this book: hang tough and persevere. This is not easy to do, but nothing worth while in this life is easy.

The vulnerability of being a teenager can make it hard to have confidence in your self.

Being and feeling accepted as a teenager is not always an easy thing to achieve. The desperation that comes with trying to be accepted by parents, friends and peers can be difficult.

It is this desperation that can blind you from the distinction of what is right and what is wrong.

A desperate teenager can get a distorted vision of right versus wrong and suicide can seem like the right thing to do.

When teenagers see suicide as the right answer, then suicide may not be far off.

There is only one way to gain the strength to get through your teenage years and that is to endure and persevere. I again suggest that teenagers please go inside of your selves, find the strength you possess and use it to overcome thoughts of suicide.

Dear Teenagers, I wish for you to live long, happy, and healthy lives. I hope that I will see you in the future. God bless you all.

A DREAM…
Losing touch
Reality at times, is to much
Much more than a mouthful
More than I can swallow
I see checkers and stripes in a sky of plaid
It's the best stuff I've ever had
Highs and lows, yet still I go
To the edge or to the top
I won't stop, no I won't stop
I can run and I can scream, everyday is a dream
Walking on water, the sun feels hotter
It's reflections of life I do see,
as life is looking back at me
Page after page, it's youth that does rage
In my dreams the rage turns to peace, and the insanity
that is my life does cease
I thank god for my dreams…
12-24-1990

Avoiding The Path To Teenage Suicide

WITH A SMILE
A different day brought a smile to my face
As I sit in a familiar place
Its funny how time fly's
If you sit to long it will pass you by
So I took the time to recognize the smile on my face
With all I've been through
    And the help of my friends, the fun never ends
    Everyday I laugh, I live, I love ...
    Like the eagle and the dove, I fly
    I fly high to touch the sky
    With a smile on my face, I fly
    Alain Tuggle   1991

Advice To Parents

STATISTICS...DON'T LET YOUR CHILD BE ONE...

Parents this section is your reality check!!! To begin with, you should have a picture of your child, children, or your family next to you as you read this section. You need to see why you are putting in the time to read this book.

This book is meant to help you and your children get through the turbulent teenage years alive.

You have the power as a parent to observe your children and keep them from suicide.

Ok now, parents take a look at your children. Take a good look at them!!! It does not matter how old they are right now, 5, 6, 10 or 12,16 or 17. Can you imagine a life with out them in it???

Go ahead and take a good long look at those faces. Now here are some sad "FACTS" …

TEENAGE SUICIDE STATISTICS...
EVERY DAY, 14 TEENAGERS IN THE U.S.A. TAKE THEIR OWN LIVES!!!

The National Institute of Mental Health says, "twenty percent of all middle school and high school students have considered SUICIDE"!!! Now go back and read those two sentences again…For the year 2001 he teenage suicide statistics are as follows:

Suicide was the 3rd leading cause of death among young people 15 to 24 years of age, following unintentional injuries and homicide.

The suicide rate among children ages 10-14 was 1.3/100,00 or 272 deaths among 20,910,440 children in this age group. The gender ratio for this age group was 3:1(males to females). The suicide rate among adolescents aged 15-19 was7.9/100,00 or 1,611 deaths among 20,271,312 adolescents in this age group. The gender ratio for this age group was 5:1 (males to females). There is no national data on attempted suicides. There is an estimated 8-25 attempted suicides for each suicide death. More women than men report a history of attempted suicide with a gender ratio of 3:1. Four out of five teens who attempt suicide have given clear warnings!!! These statistics were provided by the Teen Suicide Statistics and Adolescent Teenage Suicide Prevention web site.

They also suggest to pay attention to these warning signs:

SUICIDE THREATS, BOTH DIRECT AND INDIRECT

> Sadness or feelings of hopelessness
> Aggressive behavior
> Obsession with death
> Poems or drawings that refer to death
> Dramatic change in personality or appearance
> Irrational or bizarre behavior
> (cutting or burning them selves)
> Overwhelming sense of guilt
> Changed eating or sleeping habits
> Severe drop in school performance
> Giving away belongings

READ THIS LIST AGAIN!!!

These statistics are real!!! 100% REAL!!! Now take another look at your children!!! A good long look…Would you do anything to save their lives, or is this just something you tell yourself you would do, but when push comes to shove you don't have what it takes to raise your children? This is a question that you need to answer for your own peace of mind and the well being of your children. A parent has to be responsible and be able to take responsibility for their own actions. This is something that I can't stress to you enough.

Take a look at these numbers of 14 teenage suicides a day. Now double this number to 28, this is the number of parents that can't hold their children tonight. These parents will not attend their children's ball games, no more school plays, no more Christmas mornings, and no more birthday's except the ones in your memories, no more anything… All these parents have now are photos, videos and memories of what was. The purpose of this book is to help parents and their children avoid being in these statistics and this can be avoided when you know what to look for in your child and in your family.

As I was looking up statistics I came across this statistic: "87% of couples divorce after the loss of a child." The reasons for the loss of the child all varied, but suicide is included in this list of reasons. They also said that with the reason of the loss being suicide that the parent's divorce rate is among the highest percentage. So not only are you putting in the time and effort it takes to save your children, but you are really saving the family as a whole. I hope you can give what I've written down in this book a chance, a chance to help you get through today, tomorrow and the rest of your long lives.

WARNING SIGNS:

I'm here to tell you, there are always warning signs, YES ALWAYS. It is not a natural act to commit suicide. Suicide is a last act of desperation and it is this desperation you should see in your children. This is especially true if you have spent more and more time arguing and fighting over the years. If there is no problem between you and your children, then you need to look into problems at school, or with friends. Maybe your children don't have friends, this can be a problem in it's own right. What I'm saying here is you need to keep your eyes open, wide open, and be inquisitive about how they are doing and what they are doing. Ask them about their school and their friends in-depth and get in-depth answers back, not just glossing over their life.

There are dozens of reasons that a teenager attempts to take his or her own life. With all these dozens of reasons come dozens of warning signs. Some of these warnings will be blunt and direct; such as, if you are in an argument with your child and he or she screams out "I hate you, I hate this world, I'm just going to kill myself." This is something that should not be blown off as, "it's just your kid trying to get attention." Hear me, don't blow this off, this is your kid trying to get your attention…And you need to hear what they want, pay attention to what they want, and put in the time it takes to come to some kind of conclusion for the situation at hand. The few times I said to my mother that I wanted to kill myself, she told me I was stupid and gave me a look that to this day is still burned into my mind -- A look of disgust with me, at the time I most needed a loving mother. I needed love and some help, but all I got from her was this look of disgust with me. I'm asking you for your children's lives, don't over look this kind of direct warning. This is the time that your children need you most, for your wisdom and guidance. You need to find it within yourself not to let them down.

As for the indirect warning signs of a child that has suicide in his or her thoughts, there are still warning signs. As a parent it is your job and your duty to raise your children until they are 18. The only way to do this is by spending time with them. If at ages 12 through 17, you feel that your child has gotten older and does not need you around as much as when they were younger, you couldn't be more wrong. It is at these ages that the indirect warning signs of suicide are really relevant.

Again, I say it could have nothing to do with you as the problem. Your relationship maybe fine or so you think, but if your child, for whatever reason, does not feel that he or she can confide in you honestly, without any repercussions, then you will not hear it from your child that he or she is thinking about suicide. It is only by observing their behavior that you will be able to detect indirect suicidal warnings from your child. This behavior could be in one form or it could be a combination of many different things. For example, it could be that your child may be getting picked on in school for being fat or having bad grades. They might try coming up with reasons not to go to school, such as they are sick or they have a sprained ankle and can't walk. Kids pick on each other for hundreds of reasons, most of the time your children will not tell you this is happening to them at school. Another example of indirect warnings that your children might be thinking about suicide are the things that they write or draw. It is up to you as their parents to ask them questions if you see poems or drawings about death. Only your involvement and time spent with your children will allow you to see these indirect warning signs that your child has suicide in their thoughts as an answer to their problems.

You also need to take the bull by the horns and be direct in asking them questions and getting from them, the truth on how they are doing in spirit and in health. You know this kid, he or she is your child. Talk to them, look them in the eyes, don't bullshit them and don't let them bullshit you. I'm sure in my heart and in my mind that you didn't have children just to have to bury them because of something that could have been avoided, SUICIDE. I believe that if you are close with your children you know if they are happy or if they are having problems.

Take note parents: not all changes that your child makes mean that your kid is in trouble and wants to commit suicide. The ages between 8 and 18 are when teens start taking in all kinds of outside influences from friends, the TV, magazines, music, you name it. They may want to experiment with dressing different and changing their look to look like their favorite band, or get into sports and emulate their sports idles, this is normal. Ask them questions about the change with out prejudgment and without an attitude.

You will get a lot farther than if you just attack them for the way they look or act. Think back to how many changes you made when you were in that age range and if they act different than you did at that age range, don't condemn them for it. You need to be able to let them

Avoiding The Path To Teenage Suicide

evolve, and this means change. Some changes they will make are going to be better than others, that's just a given and you won't be as shocked when it happens if you prepare yourself for it and expect changes to happen.

I know that being a parent is not easy, but the more communication and understanding you have with your children can make it easier, that is just one more fact. I'll say it again, the purpose of this book is to keep your children from committing suicide and you as the parent have this power.

Yes, parents, I do believe the hardest thing you can do in this life is to raise your children right. Please hear what I'm saying: YOU raising your children, not your nanny, not their teacher at school, not the neighbor, but you raising your children. Children that are kind, level headed, with a good attitude, good work ethic, and good to their future spouse and children. This is harder than any job or career that you will ever have, when it is done right. That's right I said "It's harder if it's done right". Parenting can be done right or it can be done wrong.

My goal of this book is to help you go in the right direction with your parenting. Parenting done wrong in my view is the pawning off of your children to nanny's and day care. Also if you are lying to your children or misleading them purposely, this is parenting done wrong. You might be spending more time getting your hair and nails done than the time you are spending with your children, this is also parenting done wrong. I know a lot of the things I'm writing down here are common sense, still some people need a refresher course on common sense.

In life, there is no greater joy than being in a loving close family. If you need help to get the job of raising yours done, then use your head and go out and find the help. Look in the yellow pages or on the internet for parent support groups, there are hundreds to choose from. Go to their schools and talk to their councilors and teachers, also talk to their friends. I'm begging that you don't let your children slip away from you and life.

In this book I'm trying to explain to you how I felt when I was in my teens, due to the problems I had with my mother and how it came to the point where I thought all I had left was suicide. In turn I'm telling you that I know how your children get to the point of thinking about suicide as an answer to their problems. I also know that with the right help, tools, and direction, teenagers can get past thoughts of suicide. If teenagers get the wrong help or no help at all, they may end up as another statistic.

As for their problems, it is up to you to help them through them, one at a time, day after day, and year after year. I can't stress to you enough how good parenting makes good children and good people. Good parenting takes an incredible amount of effort that lasts at least 18 years. I'm asking you not to slack on your amount of time, effort and involvement as your children get older. Be there for them in their teens as much as you were when they were babies. I believe you won't regret the time you spend with them, they will not be teenagers for long. I thank you for putting in the time and in the long run they will too.

****

Parents, I ask you to be honest to your children, even if it does "NOT" put you in the best light. You need to be honest to your children. You need to think about the long run, not just saving your ass for the moment. Being honest to them when it counts will put you in a good light with them and will help build their trust in you. This comes from someone who was lied to, in my face, year after year after year, lied to by my mother. So I write this section with extreme prejudice against those that would rather lie to their loved ones instead of telling the truth which might cause embarrassment, or not put you in a good light. Please treat your children with the respect you would want. Tell your children the truth when they ask you important questions about life, or love, or if they ask questions about your family. If you are already being truthful to your children when answering the questions they have, I applaud you. You still need to read this section though.

I listen to the radio talk shows where people call in asking for help with their problems, "the shrink shows". I hear lots of parents calling in asking questions about whether they should tell their children the truth about this or that. For example, if someone in the family is sick with a disease or maybe a grandparent has passed away. Maybe your child is asking about their biological mother or father and you don't want to tell them the truth. These are the questions that parents are asking the host of a radio show, asking if they should tell the truth or how they should lie to their children. Here's another fact of life for you parents to digest. If you lie to your children, it will come back to you and bite you in the ass, sooner or later. When this happens, not only will you look extremely stupid, but you will also lose their trust.

There are some things that if they knew, it would not benefit them in any way, in fact some things may even do more damage than good. Some things don't need to be said to your children. What I'm trying to get across to you here is that each situation is different and needs to be dealt with individually with the truth and honesty. This may sound like I'm contradicting myself here, but I'm not. The fact is that 95% of what they're asking does need to be dealt with truthfully and honestly. There is only a tiny percent of things that go on through your lives that have no benefit for them to know. If what you want to tell them has no clear benefit to them, but you want to say it any way, just to get it off your chest and give yourself some kind of relief, "DON'T SAY IT". You need to sit on whatever it is and never bring it up or let it affect them, you just need to suck it up.

One of the main reasons why I came to the point of writing this book is truth and honesty. I have a mother who has lied to me day in and day out, since the age of 10 or 11 to this very day some 28 years later. It was these lies that drove me to the point of suicide as a teenager. As I look back now, I cringe at how easy it was for her to lie to me. She lied to me for only two reasons; the first reason being her driving force in life, "SELFISHNESS." My mother is selfish above and beyond anyone I've ever seen. Selfish to the bone and core of her soul, thinking about her self first and foremost. Let me tell you there is nothing worse than having a selfish bitch for a mother.

Avoiding The Path To Teenage Suicide

The second reason she lies is because she always has to look good in other people's eyes. She will do anything or say anything to look good to any one else. No matter what the situation she will say anything, yes anything, to make herself look good to others. Never taking responsibility for her words or actions is how she lives her life. I give this to you as an example, I know that all situations are different, still most of us learn from other people's examples.

To the parents that read this I beg you to listen to what I'm saying here. There is nothing more important than to teach you children to be able to take responsibility for the things they do and say. This starts with you the parent. You need to teach by your own example of being honest and taking responsibility for your own actions. If this means you need to say to your children that you made a mistake, than so be it. If this means that you have to say you are sorry, then have some guts and say you're sorry. Don't be so self-righteous that you can't tell your children you're sorry or you were wrong about something. Taking responsibility for your own actions will teach them by example. Having the respect of your children is earned, it is not an automatic right. So earn their respect by being truthful and honest, PLEASE, for the sake of your family.

To the parents reading this book, this is your wake up call. Don't take the stress and the life of your children for granted, thinking that things will always turn out all right, they don't.
This book's purpose is to save lives, YOUR CHILDREN'S LIVES!!!

Also, I want to save families from being torn apart needlessly. I am not anti-parent! I'm very pro-parents and pro-family. Having a close and loving family is what we all want in life when you get right down to basics. Please know that I'm not trying to lecture you or give you a sermon. I just want to help make more families that are close, loving, long lasting, and able to talk to each other instead of yelling and fighting everyday. What I'm hoping for is that the parents who read this can take a real honest look at themselves and their families.

Have the guts to do what ever it takes to raise your children, not let them rule you. Step outside of the tunnel vision of being the parent and open your eyes to how you are actually treating your child or children, or how your children treat you, even how you treat each other as husband or wife. The stresses of life can cloud your vision and this book is meant to help give you tools to clear the haze.

Stress is a powerful force whether your are an adult or a teenager. As an adult, you have experience to draw from, knowing that when you get stressed out there are things that you can do to relieve and get completely through the stress that's weighing you down. Teenagers don't have this experience of getting over the stress, they see it as non-stop and never ending cycle. One example of this stress your child may have is due to insecurity. Children and teenagers will always feel insecure about something. No matter what they are insecure about, the way they look, a test in school, or the big game that is coming up. No matter what it is, it is your job as a parent to get them through this stress and show them how to overcome stress in the future.

****

As I tell you here to be honest with your children, what I'm talking about here is me being honest with you. First of all, you should know that every ounce of energy that I'm putting into this book is first coming from anger and hate for my mother and I don't want your children to hate you. Hear me: "I DON'T WANT YOUR CHILDREN TO HATE YOU!!!" I'm trying to wish all the anger, hate and pain away with what I've written in this book. Somehow I feel deeply that my experiences may help you out through your experiences or those that may be on the way.

I put teenage suicide statistics in the front of this chapter. Some of the numbers of those teenagers are dead because they hated their parents, plain and simple. The reason I attempted suicide was because I hated my mother. Yes, hate is a strong word, but that's where I ended up after spending year after year fighting and battling with my mother and her lies. I say this to help you as the parent avoid this long and twisted road. This road led to my suicide attempts. If you don't get a handle on how your children feel, this road may lead them to attempt suicide. I beg you to do what is necessary to avoid this pattern of life.

My suicide attempts could have been avoided if my mother could have been honest with me and with herself. The power of honesty is amazing and you will earn respect for being honest to your children. I do understand and I also want you to understand that not all teenagers who attempt or commit suicide are doing so because they have problems with their parents. It could be they feel like an outcast at school or they get picked on because they're fat, skinny, tall, short, have buck teeth or funny clothes, wear glasses, and on and on and on…

There are hundreds of problems that come up in your children's lives where they get bogged down and they need your help to overcome them. If you are too busy with your own life to see what's happening with your children and you don't take the time to see there's a problem, or don't take the time to help them fix the problem, then these problems will then start to weigh your child down to the point of desperation. Don't dismiss these facts, which I can't say any plainer. Desperation can bring on thoughts of suicide in teenagers. It is by your observing and your time spent with them that you can help them overcome this desperation.

I've written this to help you understand how you can put a wedge between you and your children by your actions or in some cases inaction. A wedge that can last years or the rest of your life. As a parent, your eyes need to be open and able to see all of what's going on with your children. If you are inattentive to the lives of your children, your children may slip away from you, your family, and they may just slip away from life altogether. You have the power to avoid this by becoming and being a better parent. Don't let being a good parent scare you, it really isn't a such a difficult thing.

Parent's must be open-minded. Yes, I said open-minded. This does not mean letting your sixteen year old son smoke pot in the house or allowing your twelve year old daughter wear a thong to school. It just means not being so close minded that you, as adults, feel you know everything and that's that. Open minded meaning that you can allow yourself to take in other views, other than your own, objectively. Make decisions with as much information as you can get. You can always learn something new about being a better parent, wife, husband or just a better person.

Don't forget what it was like to be a kid. It's more difficult now than ever. Yes, we are farther now in things like technology, and the information we have at our finger tips, thanks to computers. The days of "PONG" are gone for good. Parents, you, have a role in your children's happiness and their future, whether you're a success or a failure in that role is up to you. It's not solely up to your children, it's up to you to help them along the way. For those who care enough to read books or take classes on parenting, this is a good start to learning more ways to talk and act with your children.

The first thing to accept should be that you might have to change some things about yourself, not just trying to change the behavior of your child through shrinks and books. It may be that you need to change and adapt to your child as well. Your children should NOT have to adapt to you or your schedule. You are the adult, act like one. It is easier for you to make any changes in whatever stage of life you are in. This is where the open mindedness comes in. Since you are the older and hopefully wiser one, it should be easier for you to accept the concept of change and changing things for the better, not just to fix the problems you may have now, but to have the ability to deal and avoid problems with each other in the future. Knowing it's for the end result of a happier and healthier family, while your children are young and living with you until the time you are grandparents 5 or 10 times over.

As a parent, you are the single most and biggest influence on your children. This can be a plus or it can be a minus. Which it is will be determined by how you interact with your children from the day they are born till age 10 or 11. After that, if you do well and are involved in every aspect of your child's life, the next years of 12 until the age of 18, will more than likely go much smoother. Just think of it!!! Having a teenager that you get along with!!! "WOW" What a concept. It can be this way, I've seen it in my friend's families when I was wanting what they had, a happy and complete family.

Don't be a part time parent. If you are a part time parent from ages 1 to 10, then I do believe that the reality of this action will be nothing but tension, arguments and fighting over the smallest things all the way to the biggest problems that come a teenager's way. Things like doing well in school, drugs, sex and the list, as you can imagine, goes on and on and on…Parents you have to train your children from the very start of life. Yes that's right, I said "TRAIN". A young dog that is trained well in the first two years will be a well-trained and manageable dog the rest of his life. This is the same for children, a well-trained child at the age of 6 through 10, will give you a great head start to a well behaved 14 to 17 year old child. You potty "TRAIN" your children, don't you? You teach them to speak and read, don't you? You are not just teaching them, you're training them on these things and everything else in life. So don't be offended when I say that if you have an unruly and disrespectful teenager, it's because you did a bad job of training them when they were in this age group from 1 to 10.

At this point there is no amount of "iron fisting" that can get your children to respect you if you have let this respect slip away by being a part-time parent. They say that "kids can be cruel." Well I'm here to tell you that parents can be cruel too. That's right, "PARENTS CAN BE CRUEL!!!" A part-time parent is someone who is around only a little bit here and a little bit there. This is one way of being cruel to your children. Being a part-time parent to a child is emotional abuse. Yes I said ABUSE!!! I know from experience that emotional abuse is as bad or worse than physical abuse. Emotional abuse from a mother, as in my case, or a father can be the basis for a child to commit suicide. I've written this book to help prevent this.

****

I was born into a life that I had no control of, all of us are. There is no control as a child and we live with the hand that we are dealt, as far as parents; that is not to say that the things we learn and do over a life time are "a given," they're not. We each have to strive to learn more, love more and live more to become better people. I do believe that everything happens for a reason and we all have a destiny and a fate. I believe now, that the bad parts of my life happened so that I could write this book to help save other people and families while there is still hope that they can be saved. I hope to reach you before its too late and your family implodes. There is a point that it is too late to fix the damaged family.

This book is my way of saying to parents and their children, look what can happen and how far a child or teenager will go to have some control in their life. The last control, "SUICIDE"

Please parents, I know that for the most part, all of you want the best for your children. Unfortunately, I can't say 100% of parents feel this way due to my own experiences. Just because you can have children does not mean you're a parent. Being a father or a mother alone does not make you a parent. It takes time first of all. All your time… or it should. Eighteen years of time and patience, plenty of patience. I hear parents say that they wish that they had some time to themselves. What the fuck is that? Time to yourself? If you need time to yourself so bad, why have children? You shouldn't need free time to yourself if you have a great relationship with your children and don't have a battle to raise them. This book is meant to help ease that battle. Being a parent is a blessing and you should treat it as such.

There are hundreds of couples who can't have children for one reason or another and would give their right arm for the chance to have children and give them all their time and love to help them grow up to be beautiful people. I'm here to tell you that your kids don't care about you having time to yourself. It might be a shock to you, but your kids just want their parents around. This means home when they come home from school, on the bleachers at their baseball or football games, maybe a dance recital, school play or even a graduation. I tell you from experience that you crush your children's hearts, little by little every time you don't show up at these events in your child's life. All children want, when they are young, is their parents approval and to see that they made their parents proud of them. This is all, really, it's that simple. This can't happen if you aren't around, day in and day out.

Please don't be so blind to think that everything will be alright and that you always have time to fix your relationship with your children!!! "YOU DON'T." I'm sorry to say that sometimes people leave their homes in the morning to go to school or work and they never come home, NEVER… Just a freak accident, a car wreck or yes SUICIDE.

Some things are not preventable, but suicide can be. This you should know as an adult, "life is precious and tomorrow is promised to no one." You need to treat each day as if it was your last day on earth!!! Which means no tomorrow!!! Do you get it? How would you act towards your children or your spouse if you knew this was the last time you'd have together? My guess is that you would be a lot more loving and caring. You'd talk and interact with each other, smile and laugh together. All that some people do is live and work for the future, a future that may never come. Now don't get me wrong, I do believe in thinking about and doing some planning for your future, but not to the point of letting today go by unnoticed. You must learn to enjoy the moment you are living in right now and you need to teach this concept to your children. "DON'T LET TODAY PASS YOU OR YOUR CHILDREN BY!!!" Parents, the insanity and dysfunction is controllable, but you need to put in the time and effort to make this happen. Love and the ideal "leave it to beaver" family is not just a pipe dream. It can be a reality, but like everything that is worth while in life, it may not be easy, but with dedication it can be accomplished. Bringing you a satisfaction and a pride that can't be bought or earned any other way than hard work.

I want to give both teenagers and parents or parents to be, a real life view of real life problems, and what I feel are real life solutions. No,

I am not a doctor, nor do I think I needed to be taken to psychiatrists from the age of twelve until seventeen. I also don't think that most of your children need to be on drugs (anti-depressants, Ritalin ,etc). If A.D.D. or A.D.H.D. was around when I was a kid (in the 70's), I'm sure my "jump on the bandwagon mother" would have had me on drugs like these. I believe that 90% of the kids diagnosed with A.D.D. or A.D.H.D. are misdiagnosed. I was a wild, energetic ball of fire when I was 6,7,8,9 and I still am, to tell you the truth. Don't take away from your children the chance to be a kid, PLEASE!!!

We, as a society, have changed the meaning of "kids just being kids." It is my view that we have gone insane with analyzing and over analyzing our children. It's my guess that 90% of your kids don't need these drugs, they just need plain old fashion structure, love and discipline. Structure has to do with the amount of time and effort that you put in everyday with your child, instilling values.

Love, well this is dealt with in how much compassion, patience, trust, and honesty you instill in your child. As far as discipline goes, I believe that discipline from the ages of 5-12 is the most crucial. If you let your children run rampant until the age of 12,13,14 or 15 and then try to instill a strict discipline regiment, you are just asking for problems. You may not like this analogy but here it is; Raising children is like making a pie. With the right ingredients you make a blue ribbon pie, but with the wrong ingredients you might poison yourself.

As for children, with the right guidance, education, patience, and love, they will become productive, decent people who will go as far in this life as their dreams will take them. Without the right guidance and love your children may not make it to adulthood. It is all within your power to make the right choices all along the way. "TEENAGE DEPRESSION," there is such a thing, but it should not be confused with true mental illness such as bipolar disorder and other mental disorders that often don't get diagnosed correctly. I do believe that with a mental illness that is diagnosed correctly, your child will need the assistance of counseling and certain drugs that alter the chemicals in the brain. It is your responsibility as a parent to see that your children are diagnosed properly. This means putting in the time to go to a few different doctors, to get as many opinions as you can get before you put your children on mind altering drugs. It is my understanding that if your children are misdiagnosed, and put on these mind altering drugs, this may have an adverse affect and increase suicidal risk in 2 or 3 percent of children. These are the children you hear about in the news, the children that committed suicide while on antidepressant medication. It is your responsibility to make sure this does not happen to your child by misdiagnoses.

Most teenage depression is emotional and not mental, it is this emotional depression that "DOES NOT" need mind altering drugs, in my opinion. This emotional depression needs to be handled with communication, understanding, compassion, structure, and patience. It takes time and effort on your part as the parent to help your child through difficult and emotional times in your child's life. It is in these times that communicating with your child is essential. 1) to help your child through his or her difficult time, and 2) this will help strengthen the bond between you and your child at this point in time, and for times like these in the future. This is your responsibility as a parent to be involved in your children's lives and help them find the strength and build the character to overcome emotional depression. Whether the depression is from problems between you and your child or problems at school or with their friends, or any of the other countless situations that come up for a teenager. This is when your children need you the most, don't let them down

****

It's going to take more than just the 5 minutes it took to conceive your child to teach your children how to behave, be respectful, and how to just be a good person. It's going to take "TIME," your time, not some of your time, but all of your time. Yes that's right, I said all of your time. From birth to 18 years old, all your time. I'm here to tell you, from experience, that all your children want is for you to be around and have your time, not just the obvious birthday or Thanksgiving, but when they come home from school. "Be Around," do you get it? Spend your time with your children. This is one of the most valuable things that I want to bring to your attention. What did you become parents for, if not to spend time with your children??? You, as parents, as someone with experience under your belt, you of all people, should know that time is flying. There's no way to harness it or slow it down. "Time is flying," and if you don't spend the time you have with your children "NOW," they won't always be children. Grasp that fact and start spending more time with your children.

I have to tell you that there are times that your teenagers don't want you around. This happens when you have raised the bar of expectation too high and they feel no matter what they do, they will never get your approval because whatever it is they are doing is not good enough for you or not done to your satisfaction. Whether it is about how they are doing in school or their performance on the baseball or football team. It could be how they do in dance class or how they acted in the school play, whatever it is that they do, it's all the same. You, yes you, their parent, have put a fear in them, giving them this feeling that whatever it is they do, it's not good enough. You may never praise them for what they have accomplished or tell them how well they did in whatever event they participated in. You may just go at them with an attitude, telling them how they messed up and how they should have done better, perhaps, never accepting what they've done as an accomplishment or giving them praise. You may only hit them with what they should have done differently and how what they did do wasn't good enough.

You, as parents, have to accept that not all of your children will score a touch down or hit a home run in the big game. Your children may never win a spelling bee or have a 4.0 grade point average in school. If you give them a complex or make them feel like losers because they don't reach your high expectations, in short, you make them feel like failures. If you do this time and time again as they are 7 to 11, then you "WILL" have teenagers who really don't want you around, ever.

Answer this question, if you do treat them how I just explained above, then why would they want you around? Parents, you need to support your children, not tear them down. If you do tear them down over and over in their youth, then I can only give you this guarantee: as they get older, they will never want you around, ever. Don't be so blind and self-righteous to think that there will not be any consequences to your actions. There are always consequences to everything you do in life, whether it be good or bad, there are consequences. Sometimes these consequences are severe and permanent. You can be the one who puts a wedge between you and your children -- a wedge that lasts forever. I hope you hear what I'm saying to you throughout this book. My mission is to help you do what it takes to avoid this wedge.

The time you spend with them also means involvement. Yes, I know that you have jobs and other things that you need to do. This does not mean cheat your children of your time and involvement in their lives. You need to put yourself in their shoes and see things from their point of view, not just one day here or there but all the time. I think one of the best ways to be involved is to have designated family time. You should start off the day by all having breakfast together and talk about the day ahead of you. Or have a family dinner every night discussing what happened during the day. Not just one morning a week or one evening, but EVERY DAY. This is one way to start being involved. If you feel that you can't find the time to do this, than I say to you "BULLSHIT." Don't make excuses to justify your laziness. You had children, don't make them pay the price of having lazy parents. Having a family takes your time and involvement, there is no way around it. So tighten your belt, dig down deep and parent, the lives of your children depend on you.

I feel very deeply that when some parents read this, they will say to themselves, "I see myself in this book." I know it's hard to look at yourself as an unfit parent or as an unfit person. I'm not saying you're an unfit parent unless you "DON'T" see the warning signs and your child attempts or completes an act of suicide. I believe that most parents start out with all the best intentions when they have children, but this does not mean that you know everything about being a parent. An unfit parent, in my eyes, is the type of person who thinks they know it all, and they have no need and no room for improvement in their lives.

Since you've gotten this far in the reading of this book, I believe that you have what it takes to take in and learn as much information to help you as a parent, as a person and as a family. You need to be able to look at yourself from the outside, as others see you, not just how you see yourself. Being honest with yourself and truthful to your family is the first step and the most important one. The moment you start accepting your own lies and mistruths, or just your stupid little problems, (and letting this cloud your judgment), this is when, as a parent and a person, you start sliding down a slippery slope from which there is almost no return. The moment you feel that you are "ABOVE" being the problem in the relationship is the moment that you are the problem in the relationship. Whether that relationship is parent to child, spouse to spouse or friend to friend. We all are not perfect and we all have room for improvement… some more than others. Again I say to you that you are the older one here and with that comes experience and responsibility. It is this experience and responsibility that should enable you to see a problem and make the necessary changes to overcome the it. For the greater good of the family, don't add fuel to the fire by being stubborn and unwilling to change.

****

"ACCEPTANCE"

Acceptance is a hard thing to conquer. This book is the biggest step I've taken in my acceptance of dealing with the mother I have and not ever being able to get the mother I wished for or needed in my life. To accept this fact is the hardest thing I've ever had to do. I'm doing it, as I write these words. Accepting that I have a selfish, self centered person for a mother, whose first concern in life is to herself and not her children. As it comes to light, from my understanding, she is this way because of being the baby in the family. The youngest child of five or six children, who was always spoiled and rescued by her family. Parents need to take note of this, 'SPOILED BRATS MAKE LOUSY PARENTS!!!" Spoil your kids when they are young 5,6,7,8 and you have created a pattern and a habit of things that they will expect to come and keep coming over a lifetime. When they are 15 to 17 and you decide to put the brakes on this "spoiling," your "leave it to beaver" house will become a war zone. For those of you who don't put the brakes on and just keep spoiling your kids, giving them whatever they want until they're 18 and beyond, you are teaching them "NOTHING" about parenting, being a parent, or just being a responsible person. "Nothing!!!"

I want to help parents understand that your children are little individual people, each with their own individual personalities as different as all the people that are in this world, just as you know people in your life with different personalities. Some people you like and some you dislike or maybe even can't stand. This also goes for your children. Some of you parents will automatically get along, fall in love with and adore you children's personality. Some of you will not automatically like your children's personality. This means you, "YES YOU," will have to adjust yourself to "ACCEPT" their personality for what it is and not try to change it to what you want or wish their personality to be. It is not your child's responsibility to adjust to your personality. You are the adult, you need to be the one to adjust and accept them for what they are, who they are, and not condemn them for their personality. This is especially important if you have more than one child. You may like one child's personality over the others. This happens, so please don't dismiss this fact. You may not even know that you are doing this. I ask you to take a real good look at how you are acting towards your children. If you do see yourself favoring one child over the other because of personality differences, you need to dig down deep inside yourself and stop doing it. Your children don't have the ability to comprehend this "difference in personality" thing. They just see it as you love the other child more than them. This is how they perceive it. This, in itself, could drive your child to suicide!!! Don't dismiss this fact either, please. That is why you, as the adult, have to understand this kind of situation and take actions to mend it even if this means that you have to change something that you have in your personality. Do it to save your family from turmoil.

Children that feel emotionally abused may take their own lives to stop the pain. Yes pain -- pain from feeling rejected by their own mother or father and they don't even now why. This is why I say that you need to take a serious long look at what is happening in your family. Take what steps are necessary to save your family and be a parent. Parents, your children shouldn't have to work on getting your attention. Don't let your child's suicide be your wake up call to the fact that they are trying to get your attention. I'm telling you again, they will attempt or commit suicide to get your attention. I'm begging you not to let this happen!!! You have the power to keep your children alive for today, tomorrow, and I pray for a happy, healthy long future.

Some of the problems between you and your children are brought on by you and your actions. Please don't dismiss this fact. Whether it be by you putting excessive pressure on them, like school or work, or you divorcing one person after another, you need to stop and look at what your choices are doing to your children.

One of the worst things that you can do as a parent is burden your children with your problems. As a parent and as a person, we all have problems and things that come up in our lives. These problems are yours to deal with and not for you to burden your children with. They are your children, not your best friend or confidant for you to cry on their shoulder. You need not talk to them about your problems at work or your bills. You need to be a monument of strength and power to your children, or at least act like it.

Now for the biggest thing that you burden your children with, "DIVORCE!!!" Divorce is. in my opinion, hands down, the biggest burden you put on your children. Divorce is not only killing families, but it is killing your children's happiness and chance for a "normal childhood." The stability of an intact family is the foundation that children build their lives upon. When you get a divorce, you start to tear this foundation down and I don't care at what age your children. You do further damage by tossing your children back and forth from house to house every week or every other weekend making them feel like visitors in their own family. When you badmouth your former spouse in front of your children or you try undermine the authority of your spouse when it is your turn to have the children, this is damaging to them. STOP, take a look at what you are doing to your children because you could not keep the vows that you made when you got married.

The bringing of new loves into your life, either new boyfriends or girlfriends, or new husbands and wives, is also a huge burden you put on your children for many reasons. One reason being that your children need your time and attention, but all your spare time is now devoted to your new lust interest. Your children should not have to compete with anyone to get your attention. If you start having more children with your new husband or wife, 9 times out of 10, you will further alienate your children. Also, don't expect your children to love your new husband or wife like you do and don't pressure them to be friends with them. These people are your choice to be around and your children are forced to endure them. How would you like it if the tables were turned and you were forced to be around people that you don't know or don't like? You need to stop doing things in your lives, without thinking about the consequences of your actions on your children. Your children really don't care about your love life, they just want you, their mother or father to be around and be involved in their lives. Divorce turns your children's world and their lives up side down. Don't do further damage to your relationship with your child by bringing girl or boyfriends in and out of your life constantly. This does not do anything good for your relationship with your child, it just adds chaos.

You need to accept that you, yes you, might be the one damaging your children. You also need to know that you have the power to reverse this damage that you are inflicting on your children. Yes, this is in your power and it is a combination of honesty, patience and time spent with your children. Acceptance about how you treat your children and taking the steps you need to take, with the goal of being a better parent in mind, will take you a long way. I know that it is hard to change, but keep in mind that you are doing this to keep harmony in your family.

On top of all of this, if you send your children to "SHRINKS" and "BEHAVIORAL SPECAILISTS" to "FIX THEM" and you don't go yourself, you will never get any kind of results. The anger and frustration that is in your child or teenager may be caused directly by your actions. It is up to you to find a solution. Make this your burden, not your child's. Parents need to look at the total picture and know what kind of family you want. Do you want to battle with your children over every little thing? Or do you want a loving, close family? You need to answer this question for yourself.

****

Some of the abilities we have as humans are genetic, passed down from our parents and grandparents through DNA, such as athletic ability, musical or artistic talent. Parenting is not one of them. Parenting is learned through many ways. First and foremost is the way we were brought up by our parents. This has the most influence just because of the amount of time we spend or don't spend with our parents, but I'm here to tell you that this is not the only way parenting is learned and I'm sure you know this already. Still sometimes the obvious has to be said.

When I was 7,8,and 9 years old, I first started to see how the parents of my friends treated them and their brothers and/or sisters. This was always difficult for me as I look back on that time now. I was comparing my family and home life to theirs all the time, wishing for what I saw in their family that I did not have in mine. This is when I started to see parenting in a different light. My mother was one kind of parent. My friends all had a different kind of mother for a parent. Being so young, I didn't know what to make of this and I didn't know that I would have the same on going problems with my mother for the rest of my life. Some things you just learn in time, if you're lucky, a short time (or less than 30 years anyway). Watching my friend's parents at that time in my life and over the years, it has become clear to me that I learned much more from them than I ever learned from my own mother. Everything my mother did was a lesson in what not to do as a parent and as a person. I don't want your children to look at you the way I look at my mother, with hatred and no respect.

I believe the more involved you are with your children at home, in school, in sports, music, etc... and their friends, you will know your child better. You will have more influence and as things go on you'll generally have a better relationship with your children from youth through the rest of your lives. This is the mission of this book.

I tried to kill my self twice at 16 and once at 17. I did this though I didn't really want to die. I wanted my mother to think every day for the rest of her life that I killed myself because I hated her. I wrote notes saying things to that fact. The years before these attempts on my life, I gave plenty of warnings. These were my insane attempts at getting my mother's attention. It sounds insane to kill myself in order to hurt my mother, yet this is where some kids are at:

SUICIDE AS A LAST ACT OF CONTROL!

I'm here to tell you that TEENAGE SUICIDE does not happen over one bad night or bad report card, it comes over some time. A level-headed kid does not just kill him or herself one day. Thoughts of suicide come over a length of time, months and years. If a kid has gotten to this to this point, there have been some warning signs along the way somewhere. This I guarantee.

Let me remind you or inform you again, if you don't know by now, suicide is not a natural act. The only animals on this earth that kill themselves, on purpose, because they are having emotional problems, ARE HUMANS. Your children really don't want to die, they just don't see a tomorrow because of the situation they're in today. That's right, I'll say it again "Your kids really don't want to die." This is their last ditch effort to get your attention. This book is about doing anything, yes I said "ANYTHING," to get your kids to have a reason to get through today and on to tomorrow.

Parents, I beg you to consider the outcome of all your actions and interactions with your children. I want you to understand that there are, at times, "PERMANENT" consequences to the things that you say and do with your children. What I mean here is, think before you speak. I'd like to ask parents to do a few things to help keep your relationship with your children alive. One of these things is to think about what you say to your children before you blurt, or scream it out at them. There are things that you can say, which can't be unsaid. Things said in haste, anger, or disgust, once said, is too late. Then there can be no amount of saying I'm sorry or I didn't mean what I said. There's nothing you can say to erase what you've said. You can say these things only once to your child's face and they are burned into their memory forever. You need to think before you speak. I'm sure you think and rethink things you say to your boss. You don't just walk up and say, give me a raise asshole! Do you? So don't just walk up to your children and give them shit for one reason or another without thinking ahead of time what outcome you are looking to reap. This is very important, not just with your children, but with everyone you come in contact with in you life's travels.

HERE'S ONE EXAMPLE:

One day when I was 12 or 13 years old, I was driving in the car with my mother and my sister (who is 6 years younger than I am). We were going to L.A. to go to another interview for acting in commercials or movies. My mother tried to make us both child stars. In the car, on the way we got into an argument, one of the thousands we've had over the years. I don't even remember what the argument was about, but, to this day, I do remember the comment she yelled at us, "If I didn't have you kids, I wouldn't have any of these problems, God damn it!" This happened almost thirty years ago and I still remember it as if it happened TODAY. Yes, she did say she was sorry and that she didn't mean it. I believe this to be "BULLSHIT," I'm a firm believer in meaning what you say, whether in day to day conversation or in anger. If you truly never wanted to say whatever it is that you're now saying you didn't mean to say, you never would have said it in the first place. Don't bullshit your kids, they're not that stupid.

I'd also like to bring to your attention something else that can scar your children, which is the way that you talk to them being a real plus or a minus in your parent and child relationship. Talking down to your children and demeaning them in public, in front of their friends, or in the private surroundings of your home is something that should never be done. The act of calling your children names such as stupid, idiot, dummy, ugly, fat, brat, and on and on is child abuse. That's right, child abuse, the constant prodding and poking of your children with this verbal abuse "stick" will only do harm. Sometimes this harm affects them so deeply that it lasts the rest of their lives. You, as parents, need to encourage your children, not tear them down with hateful words. Telling your children time and time again that they are not good enough or not smart enough, if this gives you some kind of power that you need to feel superior over them, then to you I say "Fuck You!" I say this for me and on behalf of your children who you have made feel inferior with the way you speak to them. I also believe that if you talk to your children in this manor, year after year as young children and through their teens, I believe that they will turn it around on you when they are in their mid and late teens. They will talk to you and treat you in the same manner. I believe that this can be avoided by your treating them with respect.

I think you get what you give. If you give love, you get love back. If you give respect, you get respect back. Even when you need to discipline your children at the height of tension and aggravation, even at that point, you need to understand how and what you say to your children should be done with respect. I believe in discipline to teach children respect, but there is a right way and a wrong way to discipline in order to get the outcome you desire. Please listen to me when I say that you get the outcome you desire, just by thinking things through and first deciding on what you want as an outcome when you deal with your children. This gives you a goal and clarity all at the same time. Calling your children names and belittling them is not a form of discipline in my book. IT'S "ABUSE."

RESPECT- RESPECT- RESPECT- RESPECT- RESPECT

That's right, I said respect. You want it from your husband, wife, children, boss, family and friends. Understand that you will never get respect without giving respect in return. This goes for you and your children. You need to respect your children and teach them how to respect you. If you don't respect your children, but you expect respect from them, "FORGET IT." If you do this, you are just fighting a losing battle. RESPECT… Give it and you will get it in return.

****

I'd like to bring some other things to the surface. Keep in mind that your children will be reading this section of the book also, so here we go…In my view there are two kinds of families, the first kind is:

A man that has not ever been married and has no children out of wedlock. He then marries a woman who has never been married and has no children out of wedlock either. Then they have children together and they stay together, raising their children until they turn 18 and then go off to college or get a job and then move away from home. This is family number one.

Family number two is as follows:

"EVERYONE ELSE," or a "BLENDED FAMILY", that's correct, you name it. This includes having children out of wedlock, being divorced multiple times with multiple children. I could go on.

I believe you get the gist of what I'm saying here about family number two. I'm a victim and I'm a survivor of family number two. Family number two more often than not has a lot more chaos associated with it as compared to family number one. This does not mean that if you are in a family number two, you can't get through with a respectful and loving family. I'm just bringing to your attention that family number two has many more obstacles right from the start. There are obstacles that you will overcome and there are some that can't be overcome ever, in both types of families. I suggest that you don't go to war over every one of these obstacles. Use your mind to pick and choose your battles, so to speak.

An example:

If you are recently remarried and you have children from a previous marriage or relationship, you shouldn't try to force your children to love your new spouse as you do. They never will, but depending on their age they will eventually come together in some sort of relationship. Whether this relationship will be like father and son or mother and daughter, or just polite friends. Whatever it is, it cannot be forced, it takes time and honesty. I was in a family like this. My mother married my adopted father when I was five years old. This great man took me under his wing like I was his own child, he never made me feel like I was anything but his son. This relationship was the most important in my life. I thank God for putting my father in my life everyday. In my individual situation, I got lucky with my mother picking the right man to raise me, not everyone is so lucky.

I'd also like to say something to you about "SIBLING RIVALRY" of which many have heard about or experienced. Sibling rivalry is a factor both in families as well as the so called blended family. I believe that sibling rivalry begins with you, the parent. It is your job to treat your kids as individuals, each having their own personalities, likes and dislikes. There will be no competition between your children if you don't allow it.

I also want to bring to your attention the possibility of you having a favorite child. That's right, I said "FAVORITES," it happens and it is one of the biggest problems in a family. It is also the hardest thing for a parent to accept that they are doing. If this is something that is affecting you, you need to get help because you're emotionally killing your neglected child. I know this scenario all to well. This was my life, playing second fiddle to my sister, in my mother's eyes.

Playing favorites feeds the sibling rivalry like gas to a fire. It shows itself in many different ways, some more subtle than others. It could be the time you spend with your children, more with one than the other. It could be the way that you praise one child over the other. This can happen at any age (there are no age boundaries in this category).

Here's an example:

You are speaking with the neighbor from down the street and talking about your kid's school grades. Your neighbor says that her child received a "B" on her math test. In return you say that your child "Chris" received an "A" on the test, and in the same breath you say that your child "Steve" received a "D" on the test, accompanied with the comment "Steve never does well." Then you proceed to say how much better your child Chris is, over and over without ever mentioning your child Steve again. Whether you do it consciously or unconsciously, this is damaging your child, so get a grip and stop it.

Now, to the parents who spoil your children to the hilt, you are raising little monster's!!! You also have a 99% chance of not getting any respect from your children over a lifetime. In case you don't know, I will tell you now, there is "NO END" with a spoiled child. What I mean is they will always want more and never being satisfied with what they have already. It is your job as a parent to teach them to have satisfaction with what they have and put in perspective how they are lucky to have what they have. You need to teach them that the glass is half full, not half empty. They need to be taught how to be grateful for what they have from an early age and if they are taught this very important fact, it will help them immeasurably throughout their lives. I'm asking you to take time and teach them about life, not just give them things and tell them to go out and play. Raise your children, damn it!!! They need you as their parents to teach them the satisfaction of earning things and how to respect themselves for putting in the effort it takes to complete a task or accomplish a goal. These things are not automatic, they have to be taught this, too, and is your job as a parent.

If your children are young, there are ways to teach them behaviors that are and are not acceptable in life. Things like teaching them that temper tantrums and fits in and outside of the home will not result in them getting what they want. In fact, you should teach them that it will do the exact opposite. Yes, I know that kids will always want that one piece of candy at the check out lane. "Just this one mommy, that's it, I'll never ask you again, I promise." That is until the next time, sound familiar? This can be avoided and should be. Have a talk with your children before you go to the store or amusement park or where ever you go. Explain to them what you will allow and that there will not be any more than that. This way they know what to expect ahead of time. Maybe show them how the last time you went to the store you bought them this toy or that ice cream cone, and tell them that you will not be buying them a toy this time. Teach them to understand this at a young age for your own peace of mind. Plus nobody likes a spoiled brat. You won't either when they are 15,16, or 17 and still spoiled brats.

You can also cause an insane amount of damage to a child by spoiling one child and not the other. I don't mean once in a while, I mean a constant flow of gushing and spoiling one child over the other.

Here's another example from my life's archives:

When I was sixteen my father bought an R.V. and the family went on a two week vacation around the western United States. At one point during the trip, we were in Utah and my father needed to do some repairs on the R.V. As he worked on the motor home, a tiny little kitten came from somewhere and was obviously lost. We went to a few of the closest houses around where we were to find the owner. We couldn't find the owner but we found someone that would keep the kitten. This is the moment when my sister at age 10 went into one of her hysterical fits. Crying and screaming at the top of her lungs as if she was being stabbed to death. It was a one or two hour fit that ended up with her getting her way as usual. We ended up keeping the kitten and having to buy cat food, litter and giving my sister, again, the idea that you get what you want when you cry, scream and throw a fit. To this day, my grown sister has a fit when she doesn't get what she wants from my mother. My advice to parents is not to teach your children that it's cute or acceptable to be a brat.

I hope you can understand and take in what I'm trying to convey to you here. You can avoid tons of problems, headaches and heartaches by thinking about your actions before you do them. This goes for your relationships with everyone in your life not just your children.

****

As the parent, it is your responsibility to guide, teach and train your children for the future. Showing them the ways of the world, giving them a wide range of options and a path for succeeding in life. This "DOES NOT" mean relive your life through theirs. It "IS NOT" the right of a parent to force a child into a career or goal in life. It is fine to put your 5 to 7 year old child in little league or dance classes. If they excel in these type of activities that's great, but if they don't do so well, that should be fine too. Don't be an insane parent looking for the child prodigy. The stress you put on your child to be the best baseball player on the team or best dancer in the class, this pressure is not making them stronger. It just makes them have fear and insecurity about failing because of all the pressure you have set upon them to win or be the best. Don't give them the impression that if they don't come in first in everything that they are therefore losers and not as good as others. I know you know who I'm talking about here. The insane parents who put their kids in gymnastics at age 5, telling them that if they work at it hard every day, that some day they will be in the Olympics or world champion of that sport. Or even worse, and from my own life experience, a mother or father who puts you in beauty pageants at the age of 5 or 6, or makes you try to be an actor or actress. These parents are living their lives through the actions they put their children through. All I can say to you is that "YOU ARE MAKING A HUGE MISTAKE BY DOING THIS." I know because this was my life!!! I'm sure you've seen over the years, the stories of child stars who have had nothing but problems in their lives because of just this exact scenario. Some have even committed suicide themselves. Or maybe you've heard of a pro golfer named Tiger Woods and know how his father started him playing golf when he was 4 or 5 years old. The drive his father had to make him a pro golfer is what I'm talking about here. I don't think its bad to give your children ambitions and goals, to show them every different avenue life has to offer.

They need to be asked if they want to be in ballet or baseball or what ever it is you want them to do, not just dumped into it and that's that, without discussion. I think there is a point that is taking it too far. Don't mess up your children's lives because of your own ambitions. Don't force your children to do something you didn't or couldn't do, either as a kid or an adult. If you love them, then think twice about this before you give them shit for not being first in whatever it is that you've put pressure on them to excel at or win. Let your kids be kids, don't put undo pressure on them and then treat them like crap when they don't meet your high expectations. I hope you heed my warning in what I've stated here or you could lose your children's love and respect.

****

The way I see it, there are three stages of growing up during childhood and in my view, the stages are from ages 0-3, 4-11 and 12-18.

In the first stage of life, age 0-3, your children are just primitive little beings. Everything they learn at this age is just physical. They touch, smell , taste and see things physically, that's it. Potty training, holding a spoon or glass and stacking blocks are all physical training. Even all the family bonding with mother, father and siblings, this is all physical teaching and training, done with hugging, kissing, laughing, crying and all other physical aspects of raising your child.

As far as memory goes, most of us don't remember anything that happened in our lives before the age of 2 or 3. All intellectual learning is learned after the brain is more developed. This comes towards the end of this primitive stage. You need to remember that we are all animals, we are humans, but the truth is that we are still animals. Yes, we are the most evolved animals, but at the same time we are last in the scale of achieving maturity. It takes humans years to learn or be taught how to do things that most animals are doing just hours or days after they've been born.

Horses are standing up and walking within a half an hour to an hour after being born. Then they go to their mother and find where her nipples are to feed. As for human babies, well it can take up to a year and a half to two years for a baby to be able to walk on their own. As far as a human baby that needs to nurse, well you should know that if you don't put your baby directly in front of your breast, they would never be able to find it if left on their own. This is what I mean by primitive for the first few years of life. They are learning at this stage, but most of what and how they learn is just physical.

At the second stage, ages 4-11, this is when the "intellectual" learning starts to kick in. This stage, to me, is the most important, both for teaching your children and bonding with your children. Your children start out as a blank slate and as a dry sponge ready to soak up life. This is when they begin the learning of the alphabet, words and how to put words and phrases together. This is also the beginning of them verbally interacting with you. At this age, they start to put together all the physical things they've learned with the intelligence they are starting to learn. It is at this stage that you have the most influence on your children. Influence on teaching them respect and on right and wrong. This is also the time to start teaching your children "VALUES." Teach them values and respect at this age. Respect for you as the parent and respect towards other people, their friends and your neighbors. If you don't earn your child's respect by the age of 11 or 12, I believe you probably will never get them to respect you, especially at 17 and 18.

This is a time when you need to start to show your children how much life has to offer and the things you do in life can be limitless with the right amount of knowledge and education. I hope you can find it in yourself not to limit them on getting this education. There are parents that think of themselves before of their children. Maybe your child wants to take music lessons or wants to play baseball, and you don't want to spend the time it takes to drive back and forth to practices and ball games. Or you live in an apartment and you don't want them practicing an instrument for fear of bothering the neighbors. So, to avoid this, you discourage them from trying something they want to do. This is what I mean by limiting them for your own purposes.

At this age you also need to spend time with your children, a lot of time. "TIME," not every other weekend, not once in a while, but every day. Day after day, year after year, from this age 6-11 or 12 is, in my opinion, the most influential "TIME" in the parent-child relationship. This is the "PRIMARY" time to earn their respect. That's right, I said earn their respect. This is something that is taught by you and learned by them. It is not something that is automatic from birth. So if you don't earn it, don't be surprised when you don't get it, "RESPECT!!!"

This is the time to start giving them some small chores around the house. Explain to them how, as part of the family, they have to help out with things that help the family run smoothly. Whether it is, taking out the trash, cleaning their room or setting the table for dinner, you need to involve them in being part of the family. This is the job of a responsible parent. Please do your best to raise a responsible child.

OK, now we've reached what I call the third stage of childhood, ages 12 to 18. At this stage, your little children are now turning into young individuals with their own developing personalities, personalities that may or may not clash with yours. Please remember that if you have problems dealing with their personality, it is your job to adjust to their personality, not their job to adjust to yours.

At this stage, you, as the parent, can make or brake the relationship between you and your children. I tell you from experience that if you break it, the relationship may be broken forever.

It is this stage, ages 12 to 18, that your children start to strive for their own independence. There is nothing that you can do to stop this, so "DON'T TRY." It is at this point that you need to show them the responsibility that comes with independence. If you do try to stifle their independence, then you are just asking for problems. This is the time you need to start giving them more independence, but independence with involvement -- your involvement. They need to be taught how, as teenagers, the choices that they make with their growing independence has consequences. Some of these are good and some are bad consequences with lingering effects. Yes, they are children still at this age, but you know that the goal here is that you are teaching them and preparing them for the future. This independence you are teaching, is to help them be self-sufficient in the future.

Now at this point in the game, your children are becoming more independent and hopefully more responsible. This does not mean you have the green light to slack off as a parent. Your guidance and involvement through these teenage years is essential in keeping your children on track. I still say that the most important thing that you can do with your children is to give them your time and attention. This time and attention you give them will be the foundation of a life long relationship which is the heart of any family.

****

What I've written here is from my heart and my soul. I pray that there are tools here that you can use to help you communicate with your children as well as become stronger and closer families.

Avoiding The Path To Teenage Suicide

TIME WILL TELL

How long will I be alone
Will it last forever, should I hold my breath
For now I stare into the sea,
not knowing what will become of me
As I sit sometimes I cry
At this point it's hard to wipe you from my mind
So I fell in love with you,
right now I can't see a tomorrow without you and it hurts
I don't want to be alone, why I can't explain
At times I have no face and no name
It's a cold feeling knowing no one wants to be by your side
It's a cold place with no where to hide
Yet as I stare out into the sea
I know what is meant to be is meant to be
Even the times that I want to move so far so fast, I must learn to enjoy my time while it lasts
I've come so far, to far to let it go
I want to live and grow
For now I sit and breathe into the sunset
Your face, smile and beauty…I will never forget…
You touched my heart and touched my soul in ways you'll never know
How all this happened I can't explain, no I can't explain
    So I try to deal with the pain
Pain from being alone, pain of knowing you no longer
    want to hold my hand
One day I'll understand, I just have to get through today
So I'll wipe my tears and pray for better years
Pray for times I won't be so alone, happy memories and a
    warm home
Today really wasn't so bad anyway
I still pray for your good health and happiness
You know I always wish you the best
But as I've seen before my eyes, my life is a revolving door

Avoiding The Path To Teenage Suicide

People I start to care about are here one day and gone the next
So I live and learn because you can't die and learn
Still praying for tomorrow to come and to see what's going to become of me
For now I stare at a stormy sea and I know its all meant to be...

Alain Tuggle 5-29-1995

Avoiding The Path To Teenage Suicide

Avoiding The Path To Teenage Suicide

IF I DIED YESTERDAY

    If I died yesterday
    Would you have anything to say
    As a lover or as a friend
    Something that should have been said before the end
    Now black dress and roses in hand
    Dust to dust and sand to sand
    As tears cloud your eyes and black eats the sky's
    Do you have anything to say
    Its never to late to pray
    To little   to late
    What do you say to a grave ?
    All the love and all the hate
    Destiny's a cruel fate
    It's never to late to pray
    If I died yesterday
    Would you have anything to say
    If you could turn back time
    Would you have anything to say
    It's never to late to pray
    Maybe just hold me ,one more time
    Let me know you're there, one more time
    Say I love you and dream of me
                If I died yesterday

                            Alain Tuggle   5-12-95

My Life Story

I believe each person's path is the accumulation of all the things that one goes through. At first, you are where you are, due to all the decisions made by your parents. As you get older, it is your own decisions that create your chosen path.

When we are children we have little or no control of this life's path, but as we grow older, we become the makers of our own "DESTINY." Hopefully, this book can show troubled teenagers that suicide is not a path to their destiny, but the end of their dreams, and the dreams that their parents have for them. The path my life has taken brought me to this point where I had to write this book. This is the story of my life and the reasons why I'm grateful to be alive.

****

The history of my life starts with my mother being brought to this country from Israel, when she was 17, with the help of her sister, Rachel. My mother couldn't speak a word of English, or so I've been told. She stayed with Rachel and Rachel's husband when she arrived. Eventually, my mother was supposed to get on her own two feet and make a life for herself in this country.

I have talked to the people who were around my mother at that time in her life. Until my first memories at 4 years old, this is the most accurate information I have gathered as to how I came to be in this world. Within a year, or so, of living at Rachel's house, my mother had an affair with her sister's husband. At some point in that year, Rachel became ill and was admitted to a hospital for an undetermined amount of time. While Rachel was in the hospital, my mother took full advantage of the situation and swooped in on her sister's husband.

It does not seem, to me, that my aunt's husband minded the attention he was getting from my mother nor did it bother my mother that she was breaking up her sister's family. My aunt, her husband and her young son. My mother destroyed their family, and in the midst of that destruction I was conceived.

My mother became pregnant by her sister's husband, and so began my life. She had been in this country less than two years when I was born. As you read my history, keep in mind that I did not find out the truth of my biological father's identity until much later in life.

At some point, my Aunt Rachel came home from the hospital to find her husband and her sister living like they were husband and wife. Needless to say, she wasn't too pleased and threw them both out. She was forced to raise her child alone.

The information I have is that my mother moved to Los Angeles with her sister's husband and they lived as husband and wife. Confirmation as to whether they were really married or not is still unknown to me, but I do not believe that they were married. When I was 6 months old, my mother was more concerned with getting her needs met and fulfilled rather than actually creating a family that would stay together. She wanted to marry an American to become a citizen of the United States. Rather than finding her own man and making her own life, she stole her sister's without any concern for the consequences of her actions. No thought for her sister and no thought for her sister's son. My mother's selfishness remains the core of why we will never see eye-to-eye. She will do anything or say anything, to anybody, even if it means looking a family member in the face and lying to them.

When I was about 8 months old, a woman named Bonnie and her daughter, Brandi, moved into the apartment building where I lived. Brandi and I were about the same age. When investigating my childhood background, Bonnie gave me details about things that happened during my life at that young age.

My mother and Bonnie became good friends and would often help each other out by taking care of one another's kids. A few months after Bonnie moved in, my mother told Bonnie that her husband (my father) had left to go get a pack of cigarettes and never came back. That was the story I was told by Bonnie.

Bonnie and my mother then grew closer because both of them were now single mothers raising little children. It was also around that time that my mother decided to change her name. I don't know the exact reason, but she changed her name from Gloria to Michele. I mention this because it became apparent to me over the years that my mother kept nothing from her past, not even her own name. Based on her actions, it seemed as if she didn't care if I had anything from my past either.

A couple of years later, Bonnie moved out of the apartment building where my mother and I lived. Bonnie and my mother remained friends, and my mother visited Bonnie at her new house from time to time. It was at Bonnie's house, during one of those visits, that my mother met the man who, in time, she married. That man was John Tuggle. He was Bonnie's neighbor, and he became my father.

My mother and John started dating. I don't know much about what was going on during their dating period, but I do believe that John wanted a family very much. Not only did he want a wife, but he very much wanted a son.

While dating John, my mother was also dating another guy. I believe that John knew about the other man, but he still pursued my mother with the hope of having the family that he always wanted. I don't believe he was desperate, just that he saw a future, not only with my mother, but with me as his son.

I do not know all the details of how things went down, but the outcome was that John asked my mother to marry him. The only problem was that my mother was pregnant from the other guy she dated at the same time. Knowing that my mother was pregnant and that she had been having sex with another guy while he was courting her, John still asked my mother to be his wife.

The decision was up to my mother, she had to choose between the two men. I believe she looked at what would benefit her, to be with a poor, struggling artist, or to be with a man that owned his own business and could provide for her and her children. She married John Tuggle, because he could provide her with more monetarily, not based on her love for him.

To my knowledge, that was the only time that selfishness actually worked out to my benefit. My mother marrying John Tuggle was the best thing that happened in my life. From the very beginning this man, who I am proud to call my father, took me under his wing and never made me feel like I was anything but his son. I was almost 6 years old.

From here on out, most of my history comes from my own direct memories, with a few things thrown in from family members for clarity.

I don't remember too much of my mother's pregnancy, but I remember walking around a hotel in Las Vegas with my cousin, while my mother married my father. Not too many months after their marriage, my mother had the other man's baby, my half sister Danielle. Danielle was born on March 4, 1972, my birthday is six days later on March 10th. I've been told that when my mother gave birth to my sister, she had some problems during the birth and almost died. She lost a lot of blood and needed donations and luckily she received the blood she needed from a friend of my father's who had the same blood type. Because of that trauma, she had to stay in the hospital for some time after giving birth.

My mother was in the hospital on my 6th birthday. My father, Bonnie and some other friends gave me a birthday party at a little carnival playground that was nearby. My mother swears that it was that one moment that I became resentful toward her and my sister. I do not even remember that she wasn't at the party.

It wasn't long after my sister was born that my mother and father bought a house in Malibu, California. That was the house that my sister and I were raised in. All I can say, is that it was a blessing for me. Being raised in a small town, a beautiful place with mountains on one side and the endless Pacific Ocean on the other, was a blessing. I didn't know at the time how much of a blessing it was, due to my youth. I was well into my mid-twenties before I could really comprehend it, and not take for granted having grown up in such a beautiful place.

A few days after we moved, I started school in my new town. I was in the first grade. The school was less than a mile from our house. After the first week, instead of being driven by my mother, I rode my bicycle to school. At six years old, one would figure that a mother would want to be involved in her child's life. At six years old I got myself up, walked into my parents room while they slept, took a few dollars from my father's wallet for lunch money and rode my bike to school. I was a very independent kid, but as I recall, she did not have a problem with her six year old son taking care of himself. After all, it was the early 70's and there was not as great of a risk of child abductions or molestation as there is today. Besides, we lived in a suburban area, which you would think would be safe. Unfortunately, that was not the case.

I finished first grade with no problems and I seemed to make friends pretty easily. I was in the first grade when I met Mike, a friend who over the years has been through thick and thin with me (To this day, he and his family are my family). I also met Rafe who lived up the street from me. We became close friends. In my youth he was one of my closest confidants and saviors. We talked about everything. Living so close to me, he saw, first-hand, all the hell that I went through with my mother. It was Rafe who helped me find music as an outlet for my anger, frustration and pain. Being at Rafe's house as much as I was, I also started to realize how a loving family acts. His father and mother were two of the most loving people and parents I'd ever known.

I started second grade. I was more comfortable with the neighborhood and all the other new surroundings in my world. By then, I had met other kids who lived near me. I usually rode to school and back with two or three kids, though, one day, the thing that every parent fears most, happened to me. That day I rode home from school alone. A man drove by me and asked if I wanted a ride the rest of the way home. The neighborhood that we lived in was all hills. All downhill going to school, but going home was all up hill. When the man drove by me, I was walking my bike because of the steep hill. The man (probably in his late twenties), put my bike into the trunk of his car. I still remember that car to this day; it was a beat up purple Chevy Nova with a torn black interior. I can't remember everything that was said, but about half way to my house, he pulled the car over and parked in a dirt lot. After talking for a while, the guy had my pants down and was sucking my penis and playing with himself. At some point not to long after he started doing that to me, some people on horses rode by the car and startled him. They looked to see what was happening, but since they did not see anything they kept riding by. That was just enough to freak him out. He got out of the car and threw my bike on the ground. I got out of the car and he drove off. I was 7 years old. I never told my mother or anyone about what happened to me, ever. I don't blame what happened to me that day on my mother, but I do believe that if she had any interest in taking her 7 year old child to school and picking me up, I believe that would never have happened.

I can still remember the beard stubble on his face and I can feel it scraping across my skin. For some reason, I know that I was not scared at all, but I thank God that he didn't kill me. That incident did not scar me for life, but made me realize that anything can happen and to beware of people. That was the first time that something happened to me and I was saved and protected by the angel that watches over me.

In second grade, I made more friends with other kids and teachers. My father started me in little league where I also made new friends. I loved playing baseball and all that went with it. The practices, the games, the competition and the idea of being part of a team made me feel good. By my being in little league, I gained confidence, which has helped me throughout my life. By participating in baseball and football, I became close with other kids on my team and their parents. I did make many friends, but I also got an inside look at other families and how they interacted and treated each other. Even though I was young, I had the ability to watch and observe the people around me. At that point in my life I watched my friends' families and the way their mothers and fathers treated them. I compared my situation to theirs.

When I was 8 years old, my mother got it in her head to make me into an actor and a model. I don't know the exact reason for this, but I believe it had something to do with my mother being a failed actress. She tried to live her dream through me, and she started me in the hideous business of acting and modeling.

She took me to photographers, acting classes, agents. I went to interview after interview trying to get into movies, TV and modeling. I don't have any memory of ever asking my mother to get me into acting; it was her own massive obsession. I do know that the only time my mother took any serious interest in me was during that time of trying to make me a child star. Her interest was not so much with me as it was her hobnobbing with agents and other mothers who were putting their children through the same thing. I believe it was this obsession of hers that furthered our division as mother and son. At first, the modeling and acting thing was not so bad, but as time went on, it became a major problem in many ways.

In the fourth grade, I met my best friend Jamie. I don't know exactly how we started our friendship, except that we had a lot in common, mostly sports. I do know that one of the things I liked best about Jamie was that he lived on a ranch in the mountains. At his house, he had an endless array of things to do. We were never bored. We rode bicycles and motorcycles, or we played with the horses, cows, pigs, goats, and chickens.

Sometimes we'd hike deep into the mountains and go exploring. As kids, we were just having fun, not thinking about the future, but 30 years later, we are still best friends. By hanging out with Jamie I also became close to his mother, Wendy. Wendy turned out to be one of my saviors in life. When I was young, she could see the problems that I had with my mother and was always there for me to talk to as a friend and as my adopted mother. She was always involved in Jamie's life. She went to all his sport's games. She would take us out dirt bike riding. In contrast, my mother would barely go to any of my games. My father, on the other hand, was always at my games. He took Jamie and me out to ride dirt bikes and all the other things that we did.

Since I spent so much time with Jamie, Wendy became very involved in my life. I considered her the mother I'd wished I always had. My mother hated her for that. In fact my mother tried many times to make me stop hanging out with Jamie just because she hated Wendy. The hatred my mother had for Wendy was simply due to jealousy. Wendy was gorgeous which gave my mother some kind of complex and she could see the great relationship developing between us. My relationship with Jamie's mom really yanked my mother's chain because it must have made her feel inferior and inadequate as a mother.

Due to my independence and my friendship with Jamie, I was not willing to give up the relationship for anything. That was the beginning of a battle that would last until the day I left home at 18. I am forever thankful to Jamie and Wendy for their friendship and always being there for me throughout my life.

My elementary school years were pretty basic, except for the time I got molested and the acting bullshit that I was put through. As fifth and sixth grade went on, I did start fighting and arguing with my mother more and more. The reasons mostly hinged on my friends, who she did not approve of, or the acting that she was forcing me to do. As the arguing and fighting became a daily thing, I got to the point where I did not want to be around my mother. The fights and arguments were not just some small banter; rather always loud, screaming, heart wrenching fights where I was balling my eyes out. Because of this, I did not want to see her at any of my games or school functions. The worst times were being stuck in a car with her driving to interviews for acting jobs. I was 10 years old and I did not want my mother in my life any more.

Things really became unraveled when I started junior high school. In seventh grade, everything started to change. I remember a fight toward the end of sixth grade. I don't even remember what the fight was about, but I got my butt kicked in front of some of my friends. I felt weak and pitiful. Even though I was only 11 years old, I remember telling myself that I would do whatever I had to do so that I would never be that weak and vulnerable again. I started standing up to my mother more after that fight as well.

I had been in baseball for five years and I was also doing every other sport under the sun. All I wanted to do was play baseball and hang out with my friends. I just wanted to be a normal kid. After six years of modeling and acting, I'd had enough. Six years of acting classes, pictures, agents and hundreds of interviews. Six years of my mother taking me to interviews. I hated those interviews most of all. Six years of rejection, interview after interview. The interviews were all the same. I was in a room with twenty to fifty other kids and their parents. We all had the same few lines that we had to read. When my name was called, I walked into a room where I had to impress three or four people. They sat there at a table with fifty or a hundred other kids' pictures on it. I had my one minute to try to impress and win them over. Talk about fear and intimidation put on a kid. The fact that I did not read well made things even more difficult. Let me just tell you that it sucked.

I had a few modeling jobs over the years, but I never landed a role in a movie, TV or commercial. Just year after year of rejection. I remember my mother saying at every interview, "be you." So that's what I did; I was myself and I was rejected time and time again. Later in life, I realized that casting agents did not want me to be myself, they wanted the character that was in the script. Being a child, the only thing that stuck with me year after year, was the rejection that I endured. I hated going to those interviews. Looking back, it does not seem to me that my mother had any consideration for me or my feelings. She had no problem sending me into a room where casting agents looked me up and down, then rejected me, year after year. She was so into her own world; she couldn't see how the rejection affected me and my confidence.

When I was twelve years old, I had it out with my mother, for the last time, about the acting thing. My father was on my side, but he caught all sorts of flak from my mother for being on my side. From that time on, my mother really gave me the cold shoulder. Our arguments and fights became the only relationship we had. When my mother realized I was finished with her "dreams" for me, she put all her time and energy into making my sister an actress and model. My sister was six years old and became the center of my mother's universe. That was a blessing and a curse all at the same time.

In seventh grade, a new aspect of my personality emerged that told me that I was in charge of the things I do and the things that happen to me. I looked tough and acted tough, if you saw me from the outside, even though sometimes I was dying of insecurity on the inside. At that time, I had only Rafe, Jamie and Wendy, who knew about the problems I had with my mother and how tortured I was inside. To everyone else, I was a tough, "take no shit" kid with a growing attitude.

I learned part of the "take no shit" attitude from some of my father's employees. My father had a small coffee and vending business where I started to spend a lot of time. I did small jobs to make some spending money. I worked there over summer vacations and any other time that I did not have school. Two of my dad's employees were tough, biker type guys who had Harley Davidson motorcycles. Being bikers, they always had biker magazines around. The lifestyle that I saw in those magazines and the lifestyle that I saw them living influenced me heavily. I could tell these guys feared nothing and that was one thing that I wanted for myself. I did not want to fear anyone or anything, so I took that into my personality. The women who they met just because they were bikers also intrigued me. I may have been young, but I had a healthy craving for girls and it always seemed that women liked the tough guys. I became a tough guy, at the age of twelve.

By twelve, I also started the puberty thing and females became high on my list of things I needed in my life. I had an inner craving to find a girlfriend and to be around women (mainly Wendy) who would treat me lovingly.

My new tougher look and attitude had its price. I was prejudged by ninety percent of the people with whom I came in contact. That happened with teachers and other kid's parents all the time. They would take one look at me and instantly had a judgment in their mind of me. Being prejudged started back in seventh grade, but it has lasted my whole life. I have just come to accept it.

I believe that I have an aura and a power that surrounds me and intimidates weak people. I don't even have to say a word; it is just an unspoken power that is my presence. I believe it was that aura and power that started to intimidate my mother. Oddly enough, it is because of her own actions that my unknown power started to grow.

When I started junior high school, my independence and attitude started to gain strength. Being in a bigger school, I had to deal with many more teachers and students. Most of my teachers prejudged me. Those teachers didn't teach me anything about the subject they taught. They taught me there are people out there who have no soul.

There were three or four teachers who immediately liked me and actually helped me get through junior high school. I had one teacher in particular who was extremely honest with me, not just about school work, but with everything; his name was Mr. Newcomb. Some of the things we talked about gave me comfort and confidence all at the same time. He helped me gain self-confidence and he treated me with respect. He let me know that it was all right to be myself and told me not worry about what others said about me.

I took art and shop classes which gave me the artistic outlet that I needed. I had been drawing pictures since I was young. I already had an artistic sense, but in the art classes I really started to feel comfortable in expressing my artistic side. I took all the art classes that I could. The classes ranged from drawing to ceramics and wood shop. I liked them all, but it was pottery that I really took to and I still make pottery today.

In seventh grade, I made many new friends. I knew most of the kids in the school. I did have a certain group that I hung out with more than others. Kids always seem to gravitate where they feel most comfortable and accepted. I started hanging out with people who were older than me. I made friends with kids in the upper grades and they accepted me, most of the time. When I look back now, it is very apparent to me that I spent most of my youth trying to run from my youth. I always wanted to be older than I was. When I was twelve, I wanted to be fifteen and when I was fifteen, I wanted to be eighteen. I never enjoyed being young. I think it had to do with control. I needed to be older to take control of my life.

I started making choices. The first choice was the group of friends that I hung out with and I gravitated to the toughest group of guys in the school. In this group, I felt very comfortable. We all had the same taste in sports, music and girls. Some of my friends were just school buddies. I became really close to a few of them as time went on.

Music started becoming a huge factor in my life. Music that was loud, heavy and raw with lyrics that seemed to speak to me, giving me strength to overcome the problems I had at home with my mother. I started going to rock 'n roll concerts. After my first concert, I was hooked. There was nothing like the power of a live concert and through the music I felt free of the pain in my life.

Even though I had really good friends, and with my newfound love of music, I still had huge problems at home with my mother. My mother continued her dislike for all my friends and she wasn't thrilled with the music that I was listening to either. The fights became more intense and as time went on through junior high school, she sent me to psychiatrists to "fix me." That started even more battles between us. The first two years of going to shrinks, I went alone. My mother felt that I was the problem. That proved useless because, to the psychiatrists, I seemed to be a normal kid. That was not the answer that my mother wanted.

One of the other choices I made at that time was "DRUGS". No matter how much time I spent with my friends or listening to music, I still had the daily battles with my mother which were tearing me apart. Except for the times I spent with my father, my home life was pure hell. I started to look at other ways to rid my mind of my mother and along came drugs. I first started drinking alcohol and smoking pot in the seventh grade. I spent most of the time with my friends playing sports, listening to music and getting stoned. To this day, my mother refuses to accept that I started taking drugs to get her out of my head and blames my friends, taking no responsibility herself.

My mother spent most of her time with my sister doing beauty pageants and the acting thing. The time that she spent with my sister really didn't bother me because by this time I could not stand to be around her. The only time I saw my mother was at night and sometimes on the weekends, which was fine with me.

The real problem was that my mother had a favorite child and I was not the favorite child. I made it very clear to her that I felt like a second class citizen to my sister and that she favored my sister over me. She would never accept that from me, or anyone else, who brought it to her attention. There were many who did bring it to her attention and even some of the shrinks who we went to in my later teens told her that she favored my sister which was part of my resentment towards her. She would not accept it as truth or fact.

I began to see my mother's personality, a big part of which was not taking responsibility for her own actions. She also had the ability to look you in the face and lie, whether you were a loved one or a stranger. Between the ever-growing favoritism that my mother showed my sister and my growing anger toward my mother (combined with drugs and alcohol), the tension in my life was building.

At that time, my mother had the bright idea of combining my birthday with my sister's birthday (mother kept to her pattern, which was to do anything that was easiest for her, regardless of anyone else's feelings). Since my birthday was six days after my sister's, for convenience, my mother chose a day that was close to either my or my sister's birthday. We had a combined birthday party. I grew to hate my mother for making that choice. Six years older than my sister and there I was, a twelve-year-old kid, forced to share my birthday with this six-year-old sibling for whom I had a growing distain. I hated every moment of it. One year, the party was at an ice skating rink where my mother rented a room filled with twenty-five six year old girls, me and my three or four friends. That was how it went year after year, until I was eighteen.

The rest of junior high school went along at the same pace. By eighth grade, I was putting sex into the mix of things. Eighth and ninth grades were basically sex, drugs, rock 'n roll. I did anything not to be near my mother. I met Dino that year (he is still one of my closest friends). I spent most of junior high hanging out with Jamie, Mike and Dino, going to concerts and parties all the time. Whenever I could, I stayed with them so that I would not have to go home and deal with my mother.

My ninth grade graduation arrived. Even with all the problems, resentment and hatred I had for my mother, I still wanted her to be proud of me. When the end of ninth grade came, I told my parents about my graduation. My mother told me that she had to go with my sister out of state for a beauty pageant and she wouldn't be there to see me graduate. In my mind, unless she was in a coma, in the hospital, she should have been there! Her choice was to go out of state, with my sister, to a beauty pageant. Missing my graduation was the final statement to me that my sister was more important.

Jamie's mom took us to get tuxedos and watched us graduate. She then took us out to celebrate. Again, it was Jamie's mom who took the time to be with her son and me. If it hadn't been for Wendy opening her heart and taking me in, I would have felt so alone and unloved. That was how junior high school ended for me.

When I started high school, I was fifteen. At that time, Malibu did not have a high school. I went to Santa Monica High with all the other kids in Malibu. Santa Monica was about twenty miles away. That meant taking the bus or finding a ride with older kids who already had cars. Most of the time, I caught a ride with some of the older kids. I had a couple of girlfriends who drove. We went as a group, music turned up loud; it was great fun.

The high school was huge and I felt like a fish out of water. Even though I knew all the kids that came from Malibu, there were three thousand other kids in that school. I took it all in stride, but there were some problems that came with the new territory. Some of those problems were due to choices I made and some just evolved on their own.

I hung out with my friend Rafe a lot. We didn't like school at that time. The only thing I liked was my ceramics class, which was my first class of the day. After that class I had no interest in being there. Rafe and I ditched school a lot. Since I looked older, I would go to the local liquor store and buy a six pack of beer. We hung out under the Santa Monica pier and drank. After that, we'd play arcade games for a few hours and then find a ride home with someone. Rafe and I did that almost every Tuesday and Thursday for the first semester. We forged absent notes from our parents. That worked out well until report cards came home at the end of the semester. My report card had forty absences on it and my mother went through the roof. She tried to ban me from hanging out with Rafe, but that didn't really change anything, it just gave us more to fight about.

In tenth grade, the fights I had with my mother seemed to go into another dimension. I knew how to push her buttons and she knew how to push mine. The fights became so bad that, at one point, I put my fist through a door right in front of my mother's face. That scared the shit out of her, and that's just what I was trying to do. Even though I hated my mother, I never had any intentions of physically hurting her. One time, though, when my mother was in the middle of one of her unrelenting screaming rages (six inches from my face), I grabbed her by the shoulders, picked her up, and threw her on my bed, which was right behind her. She was shocked, scared, and fearful of what I was going to do next. I turned around and walked out of the house. I didn't go back home for a few days. After that incident, my mother always kept her distance from me when we fought. Even though she still screamed at me like a nut, she never got right up in my face ever again. She threatened me with military school, but those threats were just a scare tactic.

At that time in my life, I felt that I was at the end of my rope. All the music I listened to couldn't pacify me. All the drugs eventually wore off and I was still living in my own private hell. The days seemed to get worse and the idea of "tomorrow" did not bring me any relief. I became desperate.

That desperation led me to thoughts of suicide. I spent the rest of my teenage years looking at suicide as an answer to my pain. I had gone to shrinks for three years, but that had no affect on my relationship with my mother. The therapy only added to my growing frustration at the situation. All I wanted was peace in my life. Suicide seemed like the only way to find that peace.

I remember fighting with my mother, saying, directly to her, that since I was such a burden and a problem for her, I should just kill myself. I'll never forget the look of disgust she gave me and then she told me how stupid I was for saying that. She never took me seriously when I told her that I would take my own life, which gave me the impression that she did not really care if I did commit suicide.

Avoiding The Path To Teenage Suicide

I can honestly say that at first I thought I would shock her into caring for me by talking about suicide, but to no avail. It seemed as if she could care less.

Half way through my first year in high school, I turned 16, got my drivers license and the independence that came with it. I bought my first car with $1,600 dollars that I had saved up. It was in that car that I first attempted suicide. Rafe and I ditched school one day and were picked up by the police for not being in school. After being in the police station for awhile, we were taken back to school by the police. Rafe and I were in the Vice Principal's office. Before she called our parents, she asked us some questions about why we were ditching. I had never even talked to her before, but after 10 minutes I had her in tears with my story. After 30 minutes she let us go back to class. I don't think she ever called our parents.

Rafe and I left her office and went straight to my car. We went to the liquor store, bought some beer and got loaded. As we sat in the car on the top of third story parking structure all I could see was that I needed out. Out of my head and out of my life. I started the car and I told Rafe to get out. I backed up to get a running start to drive off the top of the parking structure. Rafe was screaming at me, he kept getting back in the car begging me not to kill myself. I kept pushing and hitting him to get him out of the car. I finally got him out of the car and I locked the doors. I was crying my eyes out. I did not want to die but I could not see a reason to live. I was desperate to have some control and suicide was in my control.

To Rafe's credit, he had the balls to stand in front of my car. It was as if Rafe's mission in life that day was to keep me alive. By pleading with me not to kill myself, Rafe saved my life. There is no question in my mind about it. If it wasn't for him telling me how he loved me and begging me not to kill myself, I would have been dead at 16.

I thank you Rafe for saving my life. As a sad side note, when I told my mother about the incident she did not believe me.

Toward the end of my tenth grade year, I went to psychiatrists at least two or three times a month. For the first time, my mother went with me. At that time, I had an overwhelming need to find out who my biological father was, even though I felt and knew I was incredibly loved by the man who was my father since I was four years old. The problems that I had with my mother sent me in the direction of wanting to know who my biological father was and around that same time, I had a conversation with my cousin Billy (my mother's sister's son). I viewed him as an older brother, even though we were not very close. He knew that my mother and I had problems. One day I went to his house and we had a heavy discussion about all that was happening in my life. He said that he was going to tell me something that I could never tell my mother that he told me. During that conversation, he told me that his father had talked to him about me. His father was my father and we were half brothers. He said that when my mother came to this country and lived with his parents, my mother and his father had an affair. That was how my mother broke up her sister's family and I was conceived.

Even though I said that I wouldn't tell my mother what Billy told me, a few months later, it came out. She looked me in the face and told me it was a lie. The manner in which she said it conveyed that she was lying and I could tell.

After that, the tension which grew between my mother and I started going to another level. I believe it was due to the fact that not only could I tell that she was lying to me, but the psychiatrist could also tell that she was lying.

At the beginning of the eleventh grade, my mother made one of the biggest mistakes she ever made, as far as I was concerned. She took me out of Santa Monica high and made me go to Agoura high school. After that I really gave my mother the finger with my actions. She took me out of a school where I had friends that I had known all my life and put me into a school where I knew only two people.

From the first day I started that school, I was a marked man. I had a meeting with my mother and the principal on that first day and ended up in an argument with the principal. From then on, all the teachers and students prejudged me.

Growing up in a small community, I never had to actually try to go out on a limb and make friends. It was something that happened naturally without any effort. When I was seventeen, making friends wasn't easy and didn't come naturally. The way I looked and carried myself did not help matters. I was already a couple of years into working out with weights and, for my age, I was bigger and stronger than almost every kid in school. I had long hair, earrings and a Harley Davidson biker vest which I wore all the time. I listened to the heaviest of heavy metal music as I drove my car through the school parking lot. I was not easily approachable.

After being at that school for a month or two, I ended up having two teachers who helped me feel somewhat comfortable there. The ceramics teacher and, oddly enough, my English teacher took interest in me. Because of the love I had for pottery, the ceramics teacher and I got along really well. Not only because he could see that I had talent, but because he could see a person underneath the long hair and biker vest. That helped me immeasurably throughout the last two years of high school.

Over the next few months, the ceramics teacher informed other teachers of my talent in pottery and, as time passed, I ended up spending nearly half of each day in pottery class. I checked in with my other teachers, let them know I was there, and went to pottery class instead of being in government or science classes. The ceramics teacher also taught a few other classes, so there were times that I sat by myself doing pottery with the radio on. When I was in the classroom by myself, I felt like I could make pottery and listen to music for the rest of my life.

After being in the school for a few months, I really hadn't made any friends, but, to my amazement, some of the girls in school started to talk to me. It was weird, but after I spent some time getting to know a couple of girls, I had more girls talking to me out of the blue. By the time the school year was half way through I had twenty or thirty girls with whom I was becoming a friend. I still didn't have any guy friends, which didn't really bother me because when I left school, I spent all my time with Jamie, Dino and Mike.

In January of 1982, four months into this new school, an opportunity came my way that changed my life for many years to come. Jamie's mother introduced us to her new boyfriend, Mike. He was a musician in a local rock band called Nile. Jamie, Dino, Mike and I were rowdy teenagers, and Jamie's mom, Wendy, thought that maybe her boyfriend could help us out by putting us to work for the band as "roadies." We were young, strong and wanted to hang out with a band. Jamie and Mike were not too interested, but Dino and I took to it like fish to water.

In the beginning Dino and I moved the band's equipment from the truck to the stage, then Joe, the bands soundman and technical wizard, would set everything up and plug everything in. Dino and I hung out with the band and all the people at the bars or parties where they played. In time, I wanted to do more. I wanted to learn to set up and plug in everything to make it all work.

Having Wendy introduce me to that band was one of the best things that ever happened to me in the long run, but in the short term, it gave my mother one more reason to hate Wendy. My mother hated the band and she hated that I loved working for the band. My mother tried her hardest to keep me from working and hanging out with them.

By now, it was beyond her to see that I had something that I loved being a part of and Dino and I were not just hired help, we actually became part of the band. The band eventually gave Dino and me a name. We were "TEAM NILE", and we both loved it. The band members took Dino and me in like family. One member in particular, the drummer Jethro, took Dino and me under his wing and over time he became my mentor.

By the time I was 17, half way through eleventh grade, it was as if I had two lives. I had the life I loved, which was being with my friends, a few different girlfriends and the band. The other life I had was my home life with my parents and my sister. My home life was like being in a blender. The shrink appointments were weekly and my mother was doing everything in her power to take away the things that I loved. In turn, I did everything in my power to follow my heart. I knew that I'd move out soon and get out from under my mother's thumb.

There was no such thing as having a conversation with my mother. Her only concern was to control every aspect of my life. Whatever I said to my mother was like talking to a wall. I resorted to the one thing I knew that she hated; I cussed at her. I knew from past experience that when my father cussed, she hated foul language. I realized that even though she didn't take in anything I said, she heard me when I told her to go to hell or to fuck off. Since I couldn't get my mother to react to anything else, I started cussing at her a lot just to piss her off and get a reaction. My cussing pissed her off and, at times, it made her hysterical with rage. I finally got a reaction from her and that turned into a pattern that played out the same, over and over.

Not long after I turned 17, I tried to take my life for the second time. My mother and I went through about three weeks of the most intense sessions with my new ($400 per hour) shrink. My mother told me "her" truth about my biological father. After years and years of trying to get my mother to tell me about my father, she finally gave me her story. I sat in the shrink's office with my mother and my adopted father while my mother cried and told me that she had been raped. She went into some detail about how it happened. She told me that she had been staying at her sister's house when her sister went out of town. The guy who was supposed to check in on her raped her one night. That was the story she gave me, in front of my father and the shrink, crying hysterically like someone was killing her as she told us the story. She went into detail as to how hard it was for her and how she never thought of having an abortion. From that point on, my mother wanted me to feel guilty for her being raped, as if I had something to do with it.

After her confession, the fights got worse. When we fought, I said to her that I knew she hated me and all she saw when she looked at me was a rapist. She never denied it.

A few months later I tried to kill myself with pills and alcohol. Fortunately, my attempt at an overdose failed. With the support of my best friends, I never tried to take my life again. That did not mean that suicide was not on my mind, I just never acted on it again. I thought about suicide every day in one way or another. I had to use all the power I had inside of me not to drive off a cliff or into a telephone pole.

I constantly thought of suicide as a teenager and a young adult. Suicide is not something you forget very easily. But it did slowly dissipate over time.

I attempted suicide because I hated my mother and I wanted her to feel guilty the rest of her life, knowing that her son committed suicide because of the things she did to him. I thank god, my friends and the angel that watches over me for keeping me alive.

During the rest of my high school days, there were only two things that I did with passion; pottery and working with the band. My dream of being a baseball player died when I moved to the new school. I set my sights on working with bands and being a roadie and a soundman. I never had enough credits to graduate from high school. I think that I had an underlying feeling in me that by not graduating, I was sticking it to my mother and that gave me some pleasure.

The moment I turned eighteen, I moved out of my house. I bounced back and forth between Jamie and Dino's houses for a while. I lived on couches and in spare bedrooms wherever I could.

A few months after I turned eighteen, my mother called me and begged me to go to a weekend seminar with her. The seminar was called "Making Love Work." I wasn't really talking to her at that time. I stopped going to the shrinks and I had no interest in trying to make things good between us. My mother went to the seminar with my father to help keep their marriage together. She wanted me to go with her to help our nonexistent relationship. After a month or two of her bugging the shit out of me, I finally said I would go. I basically went to shut her up. I hated her so much by this time for the way she had treated me over the last ten years, I thought it would be a good time to tell her what she put me through and how much I hated her for it.

So I went to the "Making Love Work" seminar, taught by Dr. Barbara De Angeles. I was pissed, angry and hated the fact that I was again doing something that my mother wanted me to do. The seminar was a journey that lasted three days. The seminar did not change my life, but it let me get out some anger and frustration. It also gave me some tools to deal with certain situations.

One aspect of that weekend which really helped me, was the forty or fifty other people with their own pains, problems and demons that they were trying to work through. The time spent with them gave me hope. The experience showed me that there were other ways to deal with problems aside from suicide. In the end, it did help me find some inner peace, although I still hated my mother.

The end of the summer in 1984, Dino, Mike and I took a trip to Mammoth Lakes, California. This trip was our going away party for Mike, who was going into the navy. That trip was one for the record books. The first mishap happened the night that we drove up there. I was driving around two a.m. Just before our exit, I came over a rise in the road, going about seventy or eighty miles an hour, and standing in the middle of the road was a huge deer. I swerved one way and the deer walked the way that I swerved. I hit the deer. The sound of the impact is something I'll never forget. The deer went flying head over heels into the center medium of the road. I freaked out, but there was nothing we could do. We drove on to our destination, which was only about five miles.

When we got to our campground we were too wiped out to set up our tents, so we just laid our sleeping bags out on the ground and tried to get some sleep. When we awoke in the morning, we checked out the damage to my car. The grill was broken, the hood was bent and the headlight was cracked on the side of the car that hit the deer. All in all, it wasn't too bad. After we got our wits together, we went for a drive into town. As we drove down the main street into town, a lady and her daughter, pulled out of a side street right in front of us and we crashed right into their car. Talk about bad timing, the first day of our trip I totaled the front end of my car.

After all the police work, we got the car towed to the nearest mechanic in town. We stood in the service station wondering what the hell we were going to do. A nice older couple, who had seen the accident, offered us a ride back to where we were staying. When we arrived at the campground, a family was setting up their campsite next to ours. While we took our stuff out of the RV, the couple who drove us started talking to the mother and father of the family setting up camp next to us. The couple told them of our troubles and asked them to watch over us, because we were "nice boys," as they put it.

As Dino, Mike and I were getting our stuff together and finishing setting up our own camp, the father from the family came over to us and introduced himself and his family (which included his daughter and her friend). His name was George and his wife was Dorothy and that was the moment that I met the love of my life. Their daughter, Nicki, was seventeen and her friend Shana was also seventeen. If there is love at first sight, well that was it. The moment I saw Nicki, I was in love. As I got to know her later, she told me it was the same for her.

We were supposed to be in Mammoth for one week, but that all changed when the mechanic told me it would take at least a week to get the parts to fix my car. We were basically stuck in a beautiful place with three lakes where we could fish all day, but without a car we were screwed. We did have some food and drinks with us, but it was not enough to last us a week or however long it would take to get the car fixed. So we turned to George and his family to help us out. They were extremely kind to us.

At night we made huge campfires. George came over and hung out with us. During the days, Dino, Mike and I went hiking and fishing from lake to lake. We did the best we could without a car. After a day or two, the three of us started talking more and more with Nicki and Shana. I don't think George thought much of it at first, but as time went on, he realized that both Nicki and I had a crush on each other. It wasn't long before Nicki and Shana were hanging out at our campfire at night. I remember Nicki's beautiful eyes glowing from the campfire and how I wanted to wrap my arms around her and kiss her forever. We exchanged phone numbers and let each other know that we definitely wanted to see each other again.

By the eighth day of being stuck there, Dino called his brother to pick him up because he had to get back to work. Two days after that, the mechanic fixed my car and Mike and I packed up our camp ready to go home. As we were packing up camp, Nicki came over to say good bye. She kissed me, it was short, sweet, and blew my mind. Driving, on the way home, I probably drove Mike nuts telling him about it. The whole trip was worth it, for that one kiss.

When I got home, I didn't waste any time at all getting in touch with Nicki. She lived about an hour drive from my house. I'll never forget the first time I went and saw her. She was even more gorgeous than I remembered. I picked her up at her house and we drove to the mountains near her house and parked. I got out of the car and walked around to her door, she stood up, I wrapped my arms around her, then kissed her for hours. It was the best moment of my life; saying that it was heaven would be a huge understatement. From that moment on, Nicki and I were boyfriend and girlfriend. We saw each other as much as we could and quickly fell in love.

We were together for three years. Unfortunately, I was young, wild and there came a point when things started falling apart. She was the love of my life, but I was too young to give her what she really needed and wanted; marriage and children. I was still working with the band all the time. I had visions of going out on the road, which was not good for a relationship. I loved Nicki with every fiber in my body, but I knew she needed someone that was stable and I was the farthest thing from being stable. It got to the point where I had to let her go. That was the worst thing that I ever had to do. To this day, I think of her all the time. I wish that she was in my life. A few years after we spilt up, I found out that she got married and had the children that she always wanted to have.

I often wish that I could turn back time and she would be with me again. If only I knew then that I would never find another woman like her ever again, I would have never let her go.

I was twenty-one when Nicki and I split up. My life was consumed with the band and drugs. Pot, cocaine, alcohol, pills, acid, you name it, and I was putting it in my body. I was working days at my father's coffee business and every night of the week I was with the band, either doing gigs or preparing for the next gig to come.

What stood out in my mind during the time I spent with the band, were the different types of people that came to the gigs and the after parties at the band house. There was an eclectic array of famous musicians, actors, producers; you name it, they were there. I became friends with many of those people. We'd talk and I learned a lot from them about life. They all did their part to help show me how to find a direction and a focus in my life. I took in the things that appealed to me, and other things, I just let go by the wayside. I specifically remember what one actor told me; "always live each day as if it was your last." That had nothing to do with suicide, it simply meant that you could have a heart attack, or get hit by a bus tomorrow, thus you should live everyday like it was your last, because tomorrow is promised to no one. I live my life by as if each day was my last. I do want to live tomorrow and every day after that, until my 80's or 90's, but I don't take for granted that tomorrow will come. I've learned to enjoy today. The thoughts of suicide were also fading as time went on, but there were still times that I felt like driving off a cliff.

Around that same time, my mother and father got divorced. The last few years of their marriage they really had no love for each other anymore; they only stayed together for the sake of my sister. The divorce did not affect me in any way as I knew it had been a long time coming.

I admit that I used drugs and drinking to escape my mother. I do not condone drugs or drinking, I'm just stating the truth. At that time in my life, I'd do anything to get her out of my head. My mother's uneducated guess of why I did drugs was because of my friends' influence on me. She couldn't have been more wrong. She looked outward to point the blame for anything and everything, instead of taking responsibility for her being the cause of some of my actions – reactions to her lack of interaction!

My friends saved my life and to this day she has never found it inside herself to thank them. Even years later when I told her she was the reason I did drugs when I was fourteen, fifteen and on, her response was still defensive -- defensive to the point that on my twenty-eighth birthday, we got into a huge fight while driving. I made her pull over and I got out of the car. I hitchhiked home over 20 miles.

Different things saved me from day to day. Some days it was surfing or dirt biking. Some days it was music. There were days that I would just sit and stare at the sky and draw pictures. I'd draw the things that set me free, pictures of waves and the ocean, birds flying high and the sun. I've drawn hundreds of pictures of the sunset and sunrise. I also drew things to project all the anger in my heart, like people bleeding and fire burning away the bad things in my life.

I spent most of my time with Dino because we were both working for the band. Dino and I were quite close. I did not realize the affect it had on my relationship with Jamie. One day Jamie and I were hanging out together and he let me know that he felt like he was losing his best friend. I was blown away, our conversation got extremely emotional, and for the first time Jamie really let me know in words, how much I really meant to him. It was one of the most incredible moments in our long relationship.

The late 80's are a blur to me. I never really saw my mother, except perhaps four or five times a year, even though we still lived in the same town. We saw each other on the obligatory birthday or Thanksgiving. Even then, we usually wound up in an argument. There was always an underlying tension any time we were around one another. She made me feel uneasy about myself. She still had the power to say things that would instantly make me angry.

I had a couple of other semi-serious girlfriends in the 80's, but none of them lasted more than a year or two. In my mid-20's I felt a lack of self-confidence in relationships with women. Until that time, I had several close and meaningful relationships with girlfriends that went south due to my youth and inner wild child. I know that these relationships failed because of the things I did and the choices I made. I accept responsibility for that. As I got into my late-20's, though, my self-confidence seemed to fail me with women. I was desperate to find a woman who would love me for who I was, but being insecure made it impossible. I believe, as I look back now, that my lack of self-confidence was due to the hateful relationship I had with my mother throughout most of my life. My mother told me from the time I was eight or nine years old, that she wished I was different so I spent a good part of my childhood trying to earn my mother's love. Her love was conditional.

Trusting women and believing when they said they loved me had become a real problem. The loss of my self-confidence was so ingrained in me, that even though I have women in my life who care for and love me, I still have this underlying feeling that sooner or later they may want me to be different and not love me for who I am.

One good thing I realized by the time I was in my later 20's was that I wasn't dead. I spent almost half of my life thinking about death and suicide, not an easy habit to break, especially after ten or fifteen years. I was maturing and I realized that I just may live a long life.

I had been working with bands for 12 or 13 years and I couldn't seem to make it into working with more famous bands. I was not gaining any ground on a career in the music industry. I felt like a lost soul and had no idea what was around the corner in my life. By the time I was 30, the soundman and roadie thing had pretty much run its course. My father had sold his business and I was forced to find employment elsewhere.

In one weekend I lost my job, the place where I lived and my car, all in one shot. That was not an easy time for me. Luckily, I was saved again by Jamie's mother, Wendy. Wendy had remarried a few years earlier and they took me in for a year. I lived at their house and her husband Tim helped me find a job with a landscaper. Once I got back on my feet I moved out.

I struggled, worked hard and lived from check to check. I managed to keep my head above water. I worked for the landscaping company for about a year and a half. I learned a lot, not just about landscaping, but about myself. I started gaining confidence in the things I was doing and accomplishing. That job lasted until I had a bad accident on my motorcycle. I crashed riding out in the desert and I broke my collarbone. Because of the accident and my injury, I was forced to do the unthinkable; ask my mother to let me stay at her house. Due to the severity of my injury, I was not able to work for four or five months and, thus, had no way to pay rent. I give her credit for helping me out. She let me stay there, but it was not long before she stopped feeling sorry for me and said things that started arguments. Thank God that I healed pretty quickly.

I started my own little handyman business. With a little help from my mother, I bought a travel trailer and I found a place where I could rent a spot to park it. That is how I spent the first few years of the 90's. I was a handyman and lived in a trailer on a ranch.

My life changed dramatically on the day of the Super Bowl in 1994. That day, like every year for the Super Bowl, I went to someone's house to watch the game. That particular day my friend Rafe came and picked me up, and on the way to Dino's house we stopped at the market to pick up some drinks. When we walked into the market, a lady had a truckload of puppies. There must have been six or eight of them and we stopped to look. Instantly one of the puppies caught my eye and I picked him up. Rafe told me that the puppy was mine and egged me on to take it. Something in me told me to take it, and that's what I did. From that moment on, I had a buddy. Within minutes I had a dog. I gave him the only name that would suit him. I named him OZZY, after my favorite singer at the time. When I got to Dino's house with my new puppy, everybody fell in love with him right away and I knew that I did the right thing for me and for the puppy. Ozzy quickly became the center of my life and he went everywhere with me.

After the Northridge earthquake in 1994, I hooked up with a contractor who was an old friend from back in the band days. He offered me a job in construction, fixing houses that had been damaged. I learned a lot doing that job and within a two-year period I knew how to do almost all aspects of building a house from the ground up.

During that time I met Jennifer. She was blond, beautiful and had the most incredible legs. I met her because she was moving and someone I knew gave her my phone number since I had a van. After helping her move, I asked her out on a date. To my great pleasure, she said yes. We started dating and getting to know each other. She seemed to understand me and for the first time since I split up with Nicki, ten years earlier, I really felt loved by a girlfriend. Jennifer and I went out for about a year. I knew that she wanted to get married and have children. I don't know what scared me more, marriage or children. My life was still not very stable as far as having money to support a family. I always swore to myself that I would never marry or have children if I felt that I couldn't support them. My position on marriage has proven to be a huge stumbling block for me. Fortunately, Jennifer did not hate me for feeling the way I did. We were able to stay close friends even though she moved to the Midwest.

I had to move, in early 1995, due to rising problems that I had with my landlord. I found a place that I thought would work out for a long time, but I was wrong. I moved my trailer to another property and it worked out for a while, but the lady that I was renting from became a complete nut job over time. The only good thing that did come out of my brief stay there was that my dog Ozzy got together with her dog and had a batch of puppies. I kept one of Ozzy's puppies so that Ozzy would have a buddy to play with when I wasn't home. I named the dog Fish. After we found homes for all the puppies, Ozzy got her dog Sparky pregnant again. I got Ozzy fixed but it was too late. Another batch of puppies were on their way. Things were fine for a while and we gave away most of the puppies. Then things went horribly wrong. My landlady decided that she was going to keep two of the puppies and for some God-awful reason she took her dog Sparky (the mother dog), to the animal shelter. I loved that dog, even though she wasn't mine. After a few days of not seeing Sparky around the house I got worried, so I talked to the landlady and her daughter about where Sparky was and they both gave me the same dumb look and the same stupid answer, pretending to not know where the dog was. I'd been lied to before and I knew that I was being lied to then.

When I told Jennifer about this, the first thing that came out of her mouth was, go look at the animal shelter, so that's what I did. I drove straight to the shelter. It was closed to the public that day, but I made them let me in to see if Sparky was there. I got about half way down the hall of cages and there was Sparky. The moment she saw me, she started jumping up and down and she was barking at the top of her lungs. I looked on the door of the cage and there was a cutesy little note that had been written by the landlady's daughter. The note said, "looking for a good home, my owner can't keep me any more." The note had hearts and flowers drawn on it. I told the people at the shelter that she was my dog and that she shouldn't have been brought there. They told me that I had to pay $100.00 to get her out. I only had $100.00 to my name at the time. I spent it to get Sparky out of doggie jail. When I went back home, the landlady wasn't there, so I left her a nasty message on her answer machine. I told her how shitty it was of her to lie to me and to tell her daughter to lie to me. I told her that I bought the dog and Sparky was mine now. The next day I came home from work to find an eviction notice on my door. Thus began almost two years of being homeless with my three dogs.

I started a desperate search for a new place where I could move my trailer and live which was including my three big dogs. I could live at the first few places I found, but I could not have the dogs. That wasn't even an option for me. I was not going to give up my family. I was determined to do whatever I had to do to keep my dogs. As the third day of my three-day eviction approached, I was extremely panicked. I again had to do the unthinkable and ask my mother if I could move my trailer to her house until I could find another property for my trailer. She said, "no," I could not move there. She made it quite clear to me that it was her house and I was not welcome. I asked her if I could put up a dog run in the empty horse corral that was in her backyard. I told her that I would put the dogs there in the morning before I went to work and would pick them up after work in the evenings. To my surprise she said yes.

I still had no place to live and nowhere to put my trailer. I had put the word out to all my friends that I was looking for a place, but with three days to do it, I had no luck. One of the bands that I had worked with over the years still lived in Malibu, and Jethro, the drummer who I had worked with for 14 years, was living at that house. They let me park my trailer out on the street in front of the house. Jethro let me sleep on the couch in his bedroom. After a couple of months, I still could not find a place to move my trailer and live because I had dogs. I needed to move my trailer, but without a place to put it, I was stuck. I didn't have the money to rent a storage place. I had to sell the trailer.

After a few months of staying at the band house, one of the guys that rented a room moved out. I stayed in that room until they could get it re-rented. I would have rented the room for my self but they didn't want me to keep my dogs there.

A few years earlier my mother had purchased a so-called halfway house, which was in Hollywood. She always ended up having to repair lots of things which were in violation of the building codes. In most instances, she had a time limit of a week to make the repairs or the business would be shut down and fined. That would always put my mother in a panic so she would call me and ask for help to fix the problems right away.

I tried for many years to help my mother when she asked. I stopped whatever I was doing and rushed over to help. I had hoped she would be there for me in return, but it rarely worked out that way. I still felt like I had to look out for her and my sister, even though my relationship with both of them was strained.

There were times that my mother called me crying hysterically, saying that if I didn't fix certain things by dinnertime at the halfway house, she would lose her business. So, time and time again, I went into Hollywood and helped her out. She never thanked me. In fact, she had the nerve to try to cheat me on the hours I worked. She told me that I didn't fix things correctly. Working for her just brought back all the pain and anger that I had when I was a teenager. The yelling and screaming happened all the time. Again, she made me feel badly about myself.

Then, there was my sister, who had a great track record for picking the worst guys for boyfriends. One guy trashed her car, broke the windows and dented it all up with a baseball bat. I got a phone call to help out the situation. I had to track the guy down, try to get money to fix the car and tell him to stay away from her.

Another time, my mother called me franticly and told me that the guy my sister was living with wouldn't let my sister talk to her. My mother said my sister was being held against her will. She begged me to go over there with her to get my sister. I went to my mother's house with Rafe. My mother called the house where my sister was and handed me the phone so I could talk to the guy. I asked him to put my sister on the phone so my mother could talk to her and he refused. I told him to put my sister on the phone so I could talk to her. He refused to let me talk to her as well. He started to cuss me out and threaten me. Then he hung up the phone. I grabbed a baseball bat, and we drove over to the asshole's house to talk to my sister. When we got there he answered the door. I told him to bring my sister to the door or I was going in to get her. We yelled at each other for a few minutes, then finally my idiot sister came to the door and told my mother she wanted to stay. While my mother read her the riot act, her boyfriend went into his house and came back to the door with a gun. He waved the gun around in the air, and dared me to step into his house, saying that he would shoot me if I tried.

One day when I dropped the dogs off at my mother's, she told me that if the dogs were there the next day, she would call the animal shelter to come and pick them up. She made it clear once again that it was her house and that my dogs and I were not welcome. She even asked me to give her my house key. Now I was forced to find another place to keep my dogs. Finally, I told my mother and my sister to go to hell. That was the last time I helped either of them again.

Soon after that, the guys at the band house had rented out the room that I was staying in so, like a gypsy, I started living in my van with my dogs. By chance, I met up with a lady that had a small dog kennel at her house. We helped each other out with a trade; I would fix things around her house and in return I kept my dogs there during the day when I went to work. This situation worked out for about five or six months before her husband blew a gasket and wanted me out of there.

I spent 1996 and most of '97 homeless, determined to keep my three dogs.

Toward the end of my two years of being homeless, I had serious thoughts of suicide for the first time since I was in my early 20's. I can remember sitting in my van on the top of the hill where my dogs and I slept at night. It was because of my love for the dogs that I didn't take my life.

Toward the end of 1997, my ex-girlfriend Jennifer helped me out by taking my dog Sparky. At the same time, Jennifer told me that her ex-boyfriend had to move. He was going to a ranch in Malibu and that he needed someone to help him run the ranch. That was Phil and he bred Morgan horses. At that time, he had 12 or 13 horses and two teenagers who lived with him. Jennifer introduced us. We met at the ranch he was planning to move to and the meeting went well. I told him about all my experience in fixing things and how I thought I could help him out doing whatever he needed. The big plus was that he had no problem with me having my dogs there. I moved up to the ranch within a week of our meeting. When I moved to the ranch, I felt that the two years of being homeless were worth it because I kept my promise to myself that I would not get rid of my dogs.

Moving to that ranch was one of the best things that had happened to me in years. Over time, Phil began to have a real trust in me. I am still living on that very ranch, nine years later. To say the least, it worked out very well for both of us; I take care of the ranch for him, and I have a place I can call home.

The last few years of the 90's went pretty smoothly and, for the first time in years. I had a calm within my soul. I was still working as a handyman around Malibu and there was finally some stability in my life. Phil and I got along well and my life seemed to be falling into place. The relationship with my mother during these years was pretty much nonexistent. I only saw her 3 or 4 times a year and it wasn't easy to be pleasant. The anger that I had in my soul for her was a 50 on a scale from 1-10. All the years of shit that I had gone through with that woman was ingrained in my soul. The hate was something that only grew bigger. Over the years, I tried to get her to cop to the fact that she always treated me differently than my sister. All that I was looking for was an apology and for her to take responsibility for her actions. Neither of these things ever happened. As usual we ended up in an argument. My mother's famous line that she said over and over was, "can't you just forget the past and can't we make a new start?" That was something that I could not do. I truly believe that because she had lied to me and treated me like shit in the past, she had it in her to do it again. I was not going to give her that chance.

I believe everything that happens to us in life is a brick laid down in the path of our lives. The path of things that happen to us has taken us to the point in life where we are right now. My mother asking me to forget all of the past so that we could go on with a clean slate was something I wasn't willing to do. I will never forgive my mother for the things she put me through or for making me feel like I had to take my life just to get some peace of mind.

Toward the end of the 90's, I started doing pottery again. I had not done pottery for years. I felt the need to get back into it and living on the ranch gave me a chance to start being creative again. I always wanted to make a living as an artist. I started working toward that goal. Along with the pottery, I expanded my talents and started making waterfalls and tables. Being creative again was also very soothing to my soul.

In 1999 a friend referred me for a job at The Calamigos Ranch, a large ranch in Malibu. The ranch hosted weddings and other large events. I talked to the manager about the job. He told me what he needed done. I told him what I could do and the next week I started working there. That was six years ago and I still work there.

By the year 2000, I was feeling pretty good about myself. I had a place to call home and the security of a stable job. I was also doing more pottery and waterfalls, which gave me the creative outlet that I was lacking for so many years. My self-confidence was higher than it had been in years. Life wasn't perfect. I was still working my ass off to make a living, but I started feeling like I had some control.

I didn't see my father very much in the '90s. He remarried a few years after he divorced my mother. When he remarried, they moved away from southern California, first to northern California for a while and then to Indiana, which meant we had 2,000 miles between us. In a five years, I only saw him two or three times. In the late 90's my father and his wife moved from Indiana to Arizona. I was able to drive there and see him two or three times a year, which made both of us very happy. I loved my father and I missed seeing him over the years. To be able to drive out to see him at Thanksgiving and other times during the year was great.

In July of 2001, I got the phone call that I knew I would get one day. My mother called and told me that my father had passed away. I had been preparing for it in my mind for ten years or so because my father wasn't in the best of health, but when the call came I was not ready for it and I lost it. The last time I saw my father was about a month or two before he died. He and his wife came to California to see me, my sister and some of his closest friends. Looking back now, it seems like he new that he would not be around much longer. He made that trip to see us and say goodbye for the last time. I'll never forget the last moments we were together. He walked me out to my car, we talked a little, he hugged me and gave me a kiss, then I got in my car and drove away. As I drove he was standing there in the driveway, smiling with his great smile and waving goodbye. As I got further away, I had a sad feeling, as if I knew it would be the last time I would ever see him or hear his voice. He is one of the main reasons that I am who I am today. All I have that is good in my life is due to the start my father gave me; work ethic, love for the outdoors, sports. The list goes on and on. I would not be who I am today, if it was not for that man who took me under his wing. When I got the news of his passing, I did the only thing that I could do to feel close to him, I went to the place he started taking me to when I was four years old. I went to Mammoth. We spent many years going there together and I went there to be close to him.

In the beginning of 2001 my mother had Dino and me over for breakfast and told us that she had met a guy and that they where going to get married. I asked her how long she had known the guy and her answer was three weeks. All I could do was laugh. I didn't like him from the start and it is fair to say that he didn't like me either, even though he pretended he did. He was just another person in the long line of people that made up their minds about who I was by the way I looked and prejudged me before they even knew me.

I started having a lot of dreams that involved my mother and me arguing and fighting like there was no tomorrow. I had always dreamed a lot and in extreme detail. When I was young I always had the same dream over and over. It was of an all black room with a line of white elephants coming inside. As more and more of them filled up the room, it got so crowded and full that I was pushed into a corner and I got to the point that I couldn't breathe. As I got older, my dreams went in many different directions, but there were two common themes: One theme was crashes; car, airplane and motorcycle crashes. I was never hurt in those dreams. The other theme dream was being chased, but I couldn't move fast enough to get away, as if I was stuck in molasses. The dreams I had at that time were about fighting with my mother and there were always other people around when we were fighting. It was as if I needed witnesses to the madness that was coming out of my mother's mouth. Those dreams went from arguing with my mother, to reaching out and choking her. They got really weird. The dreams were all the same for a while; we argued and then I would choke her because I was so frustrated. As I choked her in those dreams she would laugh at me, no matter how tightly I squeezed her neck. That only enraged me more, as if it didn't matter what I did. She would always be there laughing at me, never wanting to understand why I was so angry with her.

By the end of 2001, my mother informed me that she was going to get married on New Year's Eve. I told her that before she got married that I had some things that I had to tell her. I had her come up to my house three times to tell her what I needed if we were to have any kind of relationship in the future. She came up to my place and I laid it all out for her. Yet, as in the past, she only acted as if she cared what I was saying. I told her about the dreams I was having about arguing and choking her which didn't seem to matter to her. I told her that I had asked her to come so that I could tell her how I felt about a lot of things that had happened over the years between us. My mission was to unload on her years of pain and anger that I wanted her to feel. I needed relief. I told her that the house that she had been in for 30 years was supposed to be left for my sister and me according to my father. At the rate she was going, she was going to lose the house and have nothing. I told her if she did that and ended up broke, she would live in a cardboard box for the rest of her life because I would never help her. I could tell she didn't give a shit about what I said to her.

Once again I poured out my guts to try to get mother to hear me, but as always, she proved that she could care less about how I felt on that day or throughout the many years before now. My mother spent tens of thousands of dollars going to spirituality and self-enlightenment seminars for 12 years and hadn't learned one damn thing. She was still the know-it-all, the same selfish bitch that she had been since she came to this country. One month later she got married. At the wedding, when it came time for a toast, I didn't say anything, nor did my sister.

For the next year, I didn't see my much of my mother. On my 37th birthday, in March 2003, she called and asked me to come over to give me my birthday present. I went there and after the typical birthday bullshit, she told me that she was going to sell the house. She had been trying to sell the house for 12 or 13 years and hadn't sold it. I just laughed at her, which pissed her husband off and things started to get heated. I told her that since she had tried to sell the house for years and hadn't sold it, I wanted a chance to sell it. I wanted to make some money from the house, which was supposed to be left to my sister and me. I told her exactly how I would do it and that I would do it within 4 months. My commission would be $100,000 and she would end up with over $1,250,000. She looked at me and told me that she would never allow me to take $100,000 for selling the house. She then told me again how the house was hers and she had no intention of me getting any part of it. That conversation ended when I told them both to fuck off and go to hell. That was the last time I went to the house before she sold it.

She sold the house a few months later to a friend whom I grew up with. She sold the house for $440,000, less than I was going to sell the house for and when she called me to tell me she sold the house, we got into a huge argument. It was during our argument that my mother told me that a friend of mine, who was three years younger than I, bought the house. She asked me "what have you done with your life?" Insinuating that I was a loser because I could not buy a million dollar house. I didn't talk to her for months.

November of 2003, my mother called and said she wanted to talk to me over dinner; so, I went and met with her and her husband. I had a notebook in my hand and a list of things that I wanted to tell them. I sat down and the first thing that I told them was that if this meeting didn't go well, it would be the last time we would ever sit down at a table for a meal together. The conversation quickly went south. She told me that she was moving to Las Vegas where she was going to invest $50,000 in some stupid health pill. I instantly jumped down her throat, telling her that the money she had was supposed to be left for my sister and me, not for her to piss away.

Within minutes the conversation went to how she always wished that I was different and that she never liked who I was. Then her husband leaned forward and blurted out to me that I could have been aborted. I wanted to kill him on the spot, but I told myself that I would not go to jail because of that loser. I got up, told her to choke on her money and I told him that when he goes to bed at night to be grateful he is alive because he wasn't worth going to jail for. Then, I walked away.

After that incident, I realized I was glad to be alive. I was alive because my friends cared about me more than my own mother did. During most of my youth, I wanted to kill myself because of that evil woman. I realized without her in my life, I had a great life.

When I realized that I could get past my mother, I decided to write this book. I wanted to tell teenagers that they can get past the problems in their lives, even if it takes 20 years. I wrote this book to tell parents not to do things to make your children hate you. I also wrote this book to help me put my past and the anger I have for my mother behind me.

One month after I walked away from them at our last incident, my mother called me. It was a day or two before Christmas and I was working at house building a waterfall. She asked me if she could come and give me some Christmas presents. I asked her if she was fucking crazy. She begged me to let her come to see me for five minutes. I told her where I was. I told her for one reason; I wanted to look her and her husband in the face and tell them both one more time to go to hell. I also wanted to tell her husband one more time that he should pray gratefully to God every night that he is alive because I let him live.

When they got there, my mother pulled out a few presents for me. I took them and threw them in my car without even looking at them. That pissed her husband off. He said they came to give me presents and not to fight. I instantly jumped down his throat. I told him that I didn't invite him to come and said if we were in the 1800's, I wouldn't even think twice about killing him. He looked at me, then said to my mother that I was on drugs. As they both walked away shaking their heads in disgust, I told them that I did not need them or want them in my life. I told them both to go to hell for the last time.

It has been one year since that moment took place in the middle of the street and I have not seen or talked to my mother. I must say that not seeing her for over a year has been a pleasure and a relief.

Three days later, I went to San Diego to visit my long time buddy Mike and his family. I spent a few days there relaxing. Mike and his wife Teresa have always been a big support for me. My mother's sister, Rachel, still lives in San Diego and on my way home, I decided to stop at her house. I wanted to tell her about my last two meetings with my mother and her idiot husband. I also wanted to see if I could get some information out of her. I wanted to hear her version of whom my biological father was and any other information that she knew about the situation. I'd wanted to ask her for many years, but for one reason or another, the timing never seemed right.

I started by asking Aunt Rachel if my mother was raped and if that was how she got pregnant with me. I wish I had a picture of her face when I said that. I told her what my mother told me. Rachel's first response was, "that fucking lying bitch" and to that, all I could do was smile.

I asked Rachel to tell me the whole story, I needed to know the truth. She told me what I had been looking for over the last twenty plus years. The story was exactly how I described it in the first couple of pages of my biography; my mother had an affair with her sister's husband and I was conceived. It seems to me that my mother, in trying to save herself from embarrassment, came up with the rape story. Of all the things she could have said to me about my biological father, I think that she made up the rape story to make me feel sorry for her. I can't even begin to tell you how many times she used this rape story over the years to give me guilt for even being born. When my Aunt Rachel told me the real story, I felt a huge weight taken off of my chest.

All the years of being told that I was the son of a rapist, just so my mother could look like a saint for not having an abortion and to hide her despicable, duplicitous behavior. As I said before, we all have choices we make in our lives and some of those choices will come back to bite you in the ass.

The rape story was my mother's choice. No one put a gun to her head. My mother made that choice of her own free will and it is because of that choice and a few other choices that my mother made over the years, I have decided not to have her in my life anymore. That is a choice I have made for my own peace of mind.

As I continued to talk to my Aunt Rachel, I asked her a few more questions about things my mother had said to me in the past. One question was, "did my mother grow up in France?" My mother had told me that she grew up in France until she was 13 years old. Rachel's response to that was, again, "that fucking lying bitch." My mother was a compulsive liar. Over the years I was told one lie after another. I made the 3-hour ride home with an ear-to-ear grin on my face. I was vindicated from years of feeling like I'd been lied to and I finally had found peace in knowing that I wasn't crazy. My mother had, in fact, lied to me!

I stewed with the new information for a couple of weeks and after taking some time to let it all sink in, I wrote my mother a blistering email. I told my mother that I spoke with her sister about who my biological father was and from that point on I just unloaded on her. With over 20 years of anger, rage and hate built up, I ripped her up one side and down the other. I let her know that the only son she had she would only know in her memories. I went so far as to say that if I died before her, she would not be welcome at my funeral. I want the people that truly love me at my funeral and it is clear that if my mother could look me in the face for over 20 years and lie, just to save herself from embarrassment, she did not love me. After I sent the email, I did not hear from my mother for 11 months.

I knew I made an impact on her because for the first time in my life, I did not hear from my mother on my birthday. I was actually happy about it. By not hearing from her I realized that she finally heard something I had said.

In February 2004, I received a letter from a poetry contest I entered. The letter said that out of thousands poems that had been sent in, I was chosen along with two hundred other people to be featured in a book of poetry to be published by the International Library of Poetry. I signed the consent form and sent the letter back, thrilled that my work would be published.

I started writing poetry when I was eleven or twelve. My inspiration to write poetry came from the music I listened to, the music so full of emotion and pain, which at that age, I had plenty of both. Over the years, I've written hundreds of pages of poems. I'd only shown my mother and a few girlfriends my poetry. That was the first time that I had ever shown anyone else my poetry. I did not know how it would be received, especially from people who did not know me. To hear that my poem would be published in a book blew my mind.

Avoiding The Path To Teenage Suicide

A few months later the book arrived in the mail. I shook as I tore open the box. I opened the book to find my poem and to my huge surprise, my poem was on the front page. I felt proud of myself for the first time in a long time. That was one of the biggest accomplishments of my life. The title of the poem was "If I Died Yesterday." I wrote it to tell people that life is precious and not to take tomorrow for granted. The poem came about because of the many times I left my mother in an argument, saying that I hated her. Afterward I would call my mother and tell her that if I died before I saw her again, I was sorry and I loved her. That pattern went on for years and in all that time she never called me to say she was sorry or that she loved me. I was always the one who thought about the last words that I would ever say, words of love instead of hate. The poem I wrote is specifically about never leaving a loved one in anger. If the unthinkable happens and your loved one dies before you get the chance to say you're sorry, you will never be able to forgive yourself. I have put that poem in this book in hopes that it touches you.

A week after I received the book of poetry, I went down to San Diego to show my buddy Mike and his family, my Aunt Rachel, my Uncle Hiam and his family. Hiam is my mother's brother. When I stopped at his house, we talked about my mother. Hiam and his wife Margaret moved to the U.S. when I was 11 or 12. They lived at my house in Malibu for a year before they moved to San Diego. During the time they lived with us they saw, first hand, exactly how my mother treated me and the relationship that we had. I asked them some questions about what they had seen while living with us as well as how they felt about the way my mother treated me. I was able to get some more clarity and more peace of mind. They saw that my mother treated me like a second class citizen compared to my sister.

I also wanted to know one specific thing about my heritage. My mother had always told me that she was French. I asked Hiam if that was true. He told me it was not true and that our family was of Israeli descent. One more lie added to the long list of lies that I'd been told by my mother. Even though I'm a grown man now, it still pains me to know that my mother could look me in the eye and lie to me about such major things in her life and mine.

In June 2004, I received a letter from the International Society of Poets. The letter stated that they nominated me for International Poet of the year. I couldn't believe what I read. I actually had to show a couple of people the letter and ask them if I had read it correctly. I was almost in total disbelief. I called the International Society of Poets to confirm it and it was true. I was one of 1500 people chosen worldwide for international poet of the year. The lady I talked to on the phone told me that there were millions of people up for the award, but only 1500 were chosen. To say the least, I was blown away. The competition would be held in Philadelphia, two months later.

I told my friends and people I worked with at the Calamigos ranch, that I was nominated for the poetry award. They were all taken aback, none of them could even guess that I had poetry inside of me, poetry enough to stand out and be nominated for poet of the year! They were equally as surprised, as was I.

I wasn't sure I would be able to get there because I didn't have the money to go to Philadelphia. I talked to my boss at the ranch and to my great surprise, he said he was proud of me and he would help me to get to Philadelphia for the contest. He bought my plane tickets. It was one of the most generous things anyone has ever done for me. I called my friend Mike and his wife. I told them about my nomination and they were extremely happy for me. I was reluctant to ask them for financial support, but I still needed a little money to make the trip. They were incredible. They asked me to come down to their house so that they could take me shopping for some nice clothes to wear and helped me put the rest of the money together for my stay in Philadelphia. Even both of their mothers chipped in. All the help that I received meant so much to me.

I spent the next two months preparing myself for the poetry contest and when August came, I was ready to give it my best shot. I went and

Avoiding The Path To Teenage Suicide

read my poem in front of a hundred people. I didn't win, but the experience was really good for me.

In the back of my mind, while I was doing all that, my mother's voice echoed in my mind saying "what have you ever done with your life?" The irony was that the poem was written because of the pain that she caused me. I started thinking about what I have done with my life and then I compared it to what my mother has done with hers.

My mother's accomplishments are as follows:
She successfully broke up her sister's family.
She successfully got pregnant by her sister's husband.
When she was dating two men at once, she successfully got pregnant by one of them, and then successfully married the other one.
She successfully lied to me for over 20 years about being raped.
She succeeded in making my sister a princess and a liar just like herself.
She was a total success in spending over $600,000 in the last 15 years and has absolutely nothing to show for it.

That is about it for her great accomplishments as I see it.

As for her failures:
She failed at keeping her sister's husband.
She failed at being an actress.
She failed at making me a child star.
She failed at making my sister a child star and runway model.
She failed at her marriage to my father.
She failed me when I was homeless and needed some help.
She failed in her actor management business and her halfway house business.
She failed to tell me the truth about my biological father.

I'm sure that if I wanted to, I could come up with 15 or 20 more failures, but I don't want to. I am at the point, in my life, and in this book, where I am done talking about her. I am looking and moving forward.

When I look back at my life, as far as accomplishments and failures, I know that my accomplishments outweigh the failures ten-fold. My biggest accomplishment was probably that I stuck to my guns and I survived. I started with the friends that I made when I was young and was able to not let my mother dictate who my friends should be. Even though I was young, I knew that Jaime, Dino, Mike and Rafe were people I needed in my life and they would be there for the long haul. I felt it in my soul. Now, at age 38, these guys are not just my friends, they are my family.

I stuck to my guns and worked my ass off for every band that hired me. In all those years of shows, the crowd screamed praises for the band, but it was the band that turned to me and thanked me for doing such a good job.

I think of all the pottery, tables and waterfalls I have made over the years. I have sold thousands of pieces of pottery and I believe that some of my pottery will be around long after I am gone from this world. I get extreme pleasure knowing that there are people all over that have my pottery in their homes.

In my years of doing construction, I built houses that were beautiful and will definitely outlast me. There are times that I drive around and smile when I see a house that I helped build.

In the last year or so, I've also realized that my poetry is something that stands for itself. As I finish the year 2004, I have had two poems published and was nominated for International Poet of the year. That was something I never expected and to see my poetry in two beautiful books gives me incredible satisfaction which can't be bought, only earned.

My latest accomplishment is this book, I started writing it 13 months ago. My life has been consumed by it. I cannot even begin to say how difficult it was for me. I've never even written a poem that was more than two pages long. This has been the most difficult thing that I have ever done, but it had to be done. Whether I sell a million copies or five, I had to write this book.

Having to relive all the pain that I experienced when I was a child and trying to release some of the anger which has built up in me over the years was not easy. This book was written to help teenagers find a way to overcome thoughts of suicide. If my suicide attempts had been successful, I wouldn't have had any accomplishments and this book would have never been written.

As I see it, my only failure in life was to give my mother the ability to continually make me feel like shit. I should have banished her from my life 20 years ago, but you live and you learn. I have not seen or talked to my mother since December 2003. I have not had a dream about fighting with her in over eight months. I think that I am starting to work out my past demons and I'm looking forward to a happy future. I'm starting off the New Year with enthusiasm. This book is finished and I'm moving to a new beautiful ranch. My dogs and I are going to call our new place home for many years to come. I am still blessed with having the best family and friends in the world and I will never take these blessings for granted.

Because of all that I have been through with my mother, I've decided that I do not want her in my life and this is a consequence that she cannot change or manipulate in any way. As far as I am concerned, that chapter in my life is finally over and I will never give her the chance to make me feel worthless again.

I have come to the end of my life's history and the end of this book. I hope those who read this book get as much out of it as I did writing it. Today is the beginning of the rest of my life, January 11, 2005.

In Closing

As I get to the last few paragraphs of this book, I feel extremely liberated. What I'm hoping for is, that people are going to read this and have their minds blown wide open, parents and teenagers alike. Get out of the tunnel vision of your lives, and open your eyes. See how the way you interact with your loved ones affects every aspect of your life, or what happens with a lack of interaction. Whether it's parent and their children, brothers and sisters, or husbands and wives. I can't stress to you enough the fact that you do not have all the time in the world. Ask any mother of a child that's in the cancer ward at your local hospital, as her child is battling or dying of cancer. Ask her about the time she has left with her child. She if she feels like she has all the time in the world, my guess would be, NO!!! Everyday that their child is alive is a blessing to them. They would trade places with you in a heart beat, with those that have healthy children , but because of working to much or whatever, they are just to involved in their own lives, they pay no attention to their children.

I don't mean to sound so morbid, but I have known people that left their homes in the morning and for one reason or another they never came back home. Due to car accident, heart attack, or acts of god, whatever the reason was they past away. No last hug or kiss, not one more smile or saying the words I LOVE YOU. This does not always happen to somebody else, it can happen to you, your family and your loved ones. My reasons for saying this are simple, should the unthinkable happen to your child, spouse or other loved one. It will give you peace in your heart to know the last words you had with them were loving and not words of anger and hostility.

This book is about me taking back my life from the anger that's inside of me, due to my hurricane of a relationship I had with my mother. This is the start of a new life for me and a new attitude about life. I hope that this book is a tool that you will use in your life. If you are a teenager that needs help I pray that I've shown you a path to getting through a troubled today and wanting to make tomorrow better. This book is for teenagers to see and find a reason to keep living and moving forward through life and tough times. As for the parents that have taken the time to read this book, I thank you. I hope I've inspired you to be involved in your children's life, everyday, day after day until your child is not a child any more. The day will come that you have in front of you a well rounded, well adjusted , ready to take on the world young man or woman. That is respectful of you and all the people that come in and out of their lives.

There is nothing better than being a happy close family, and I wish this for all of you.

ENDLESS IS THE RIVER

In the dark, there is no moon
I've lost my heart and the end comes to soon
Flowing down the stream
Living with the dream
Endless is the river
When tomorrow seems like forever
I've written these words down with no control
Only body and soul
Down the river I flow
It's cold and dark as I feel the beating of my heart

And as I scream ,I try to wake from this dream
Running , faster and faster
How far can I go in the dark
When tomorrow seems like forever
Endless is the river
I'm running but I can't move
There are no stars to light my way
There is no safe place to stay
Only the river can take me home
The river keeps me from being alone
Endless is the river

Alain Tuggle   1993...

Printed in the United States
81066LV00004B/76